Wl *hat Kind
of *Can I Be
On

"Sharp, practical, and a pleasure to read, this is an indispensable tool for indie writers. Hutchins maps the shortest distance between you and your readers. You need this book!" - Mark Moore, writer and editor

"Sassy, brassy, can-do voice. It's very inspiring." - Martin Turnbull, author of *The Garden of Allah* novels

"Fabulous! Dozens and dozens of great suggestions and resources. Indie writers are going to LOVE this book, not only for its insights, but for Pamela's witty personality." - Jennifer Meils, writer, editor, and journalism teacher

"*Loser* is so packed full of useful, important information, it will become the Bible of indie publishing. As always, Pamela's wit and humor shines throughout. Definitely a must-have for any author." - Rhonda Erb, writer and editor

"Awesome information; very well written." - Fernanda Brady, writer and English teacher

What Kind of Loser Indie Publishes, and How Can I Be One, Too?

Pamela Fagan Hutchins

SkipJack Publishing books may be purchased for educational,
business, or sales promotional use. For information, please write to
Sales, SkipJack Publishing, P.O.B. 31160 Houston, TX 77231.

First U.S. Edition

Hutchins, Pamela Fagan

What Kind of Loser Indie Publishes, and How Can I Be One,
Too?/by Pamela Fagan Hutchins

ISBN: 1-939889-08-1

ISBN-13: 978-1-939889-08-9 (SkipJack Publishing)

DEDICATION

To all'a we.

CONTENTS

ACKNOWLEDGMENTS

A girl is nothing without her BFFs. Big up to my publishing partner in crime, Eric. Props to my editor, Meghan Pinson, for her ability to mind-meld and her flexibility with the hyphen and all its close cousins. How about that hilarious cover? Yay, Heidi Dorey! Thanks to my offspring (Marie, Liz, Clark Kent, and Susanne), mother, and husband, whose stellar driving and able assistance made it possible for me to write on the road. Special thanks to Marie for jumping into the deep end and swimming like mad. God bless my beta readers: Fern, Rhonda, Melissa, Jen, and Martin. And finally, I truly appreciate the questions, comments, and—oh, happy day—encouraging words from you guys. The readers. The writers in my workshops. The booksellers, agents, editors, and other publishing folks. You guys energize and challenge me. Life is good.

INTRODUCTION: GETTING YOUR MONEY'S WORTH FROM THIS BOOK

I'm a goal-oriented kind of woman, and I think it's useful to share the goals I set for myself when I wrote this book, my goals for its value to you, the reader.

Goal #1: To provide information useful to you as you decide whether to indie publish.

Goal #2: To inspire you to identify yourself as a writer and go about the lonely and difficult process of **becoming** one—with a vengeance.

Goal #3: To help you make strategic choices about what, when, and how to indie publish.

Goal #4: To provide you with feasible solutions to specific challenges you will face.

Goal #5: To show you the most accessible ways to achieve visibility.

Goal #6: To pass along tips and tools that will help you develop your plans, budgets, and timelines.

I didn't write this book for me. It was fun to do, but I wrote it for you. Because of "we." My Virgin-Islands-born husband uses an expression I love: "One'a we for all'a we." I'm one of you: a pure maverick, never traditionally published as a solo writer, going forth from no books and no dollars from book sales into the great unknown. Now I have nine books out, and I'm starting to see a return on my investment. No one has sponsored me, endorsed me, or given me money. I'm not a hybrid author who moves back and forth between the indie- and traditional-publishing worlds. I'm ground zero to 50,000 feet. If I can do this, and share what I've learned, maybe you really can do it, too. Don't you think?

In order to get the most out of *What Kind of Loser Indie Publishes*—which I will call *Loser* for short from here on out—I advise you to read it cover to cover, then go back and refer to individual chapters for guidance. While reading it front to back is optimal, most chapters also do just fine standing alone, since many of them were born as posts for SkipJack Publishing's indie-publishing blog.

Some of you will want to skip parts 1 and 2. I know you will. You're impatient that way, always in a hurry. But you are exactly the people who should read it. You're the ones I wrote it for, the ones that booksellers bend my ear about when I'm in their stores. You want to know what they say? I mean, do you *really* want to know? Because it's gonna sting. "In a rush, and it showed." "Bad writing." "Horrible editing." "Oh, that cover." "Might have been a good book if they'd just given it more time and editing." Shudder.

And you skippers are the ones I meet at events, lamenting about how poorly your decisions turned out for you. "Maybe I should have taken my time and really figured out what I wanted and how to do it before I signed on with [insert name of any author-service company/small publisher here]." "I have to buy the first 1,000 print copies from my publisher myself. Am I getting screwed?" (Short answer: yes.)

However you choose to read it, you'll find that this book is packed so full of information, I really should have charged double for it. Hurry, read it quickly before I change my mind.

PART ONE:
YOU CAN BE A BIG-TIME LOSER.

1 • EARN (NO) MONEY ALL BY YOURSELF

On the financial implications of traditional versus indie publishing

My personal description of an indie-publishing Loser:

—Willing to work hard to make little or nothing

—Comfortable having people whisper "he couldn't get a real book contract" behind his back

—Under the right circumstances, would run naked on a beach

Seriously, y'all, any writers out there? If you're a writer, chances are you're not in the game expecting a Spindletop-gusher payday. Sure, it would be nice, but we all know most writers— most traditionally published authors—are working stiffs like the rest of us. For every J.K. Rowling, there's a legion of also-rans slodging away at day jobs they might not even like. English teachers. Air-conditioner installers. Attorneys by day, like me, and night-and-weekend artists, like most of you reading this book.

For every traditionally published author working a day job, there are millions of writers who haven't wrapped their hands around that solidly satisfying brass ring—true writers, writers called by their hearts to lay their souls or their wisdom on the page, yet writers who haven't earned a single cent on a book sale in any form of publishing. Maybe they're already living the life, working as journalists, Hallmark-card poets, writers of jingles, dishwasher ads, and Viagra commercials, but the bulk of them aren't summering in the Hamptons.

Have you ever met anyone who worked harder than a writer trying to make a living off writing alone? Yeah, me either.

So why do we write, and why do we seek to publish, if it isn't a sure path to riches? I can't speak for you, but I can repeat what writers around the country tell me. It's the same thing that drives me, and it's easy to sum up: we can't stop writing and dreaming of sharing our work with other people any more than we can stop breathing in and out. We just can't help it. Nor can we help dreaming that someone is going to come along to take the whole mucky, scary business of publishing off our hands— or at least make it very easy.

Because make no mistake, while writing is an art, publishing *is* a mucky, scary business, complete with supply chains, distribution networks, profit and loss statements, and inventory issues. It's a business of relationships, contracts, and figuring out how to get the customer what she needs. It's a business where, in essence, the decision about which books to publish usually hinges on whether or not they will be profitable; in other words, whether they will earn more money than it costs to put them into the customers' hands.

It's a business, like all businesses, that relies on the almighty dollar (or euro or deutsche mark or whatever). Can we afford to keep the lights on and the doors open? Can we pay our employees? Can we assure the owners that their money isn't better spent elsewhere?

That doesn't sound very artistic, does it? It isn't. No wonder many of us would love some publishing company to swoop in and take away the risk, the effort, and the sheer messiness of it all. Plus, gosh, doesn't it mean you're somebody special if a big publisher takes on your book? It's validating, at the very least.

But signing yourself and your art over to a publisher comes at a price. For all that help—valuable help—you give up a hefty piece of your future earnings and a large measure of control. Make no mistake: you pay the publishing company to publish your book. They choose your book(s) because they think they can make money off of you. They provide services and call most of the shots, like what (if any) budget they will allot for advertising, marketing, promotion, and publicity. Like what your cover will look like. Like whether they'll ever let your book see the light of day without the revisions they deem necessary. Whether and which reviews they will seek for it, and what kind of weight they'll put behind those requests. How they'll promote it. When they will release it, and which other possibly competing books they'll be handling as well.

Shall I go on? I could, and it's a pretty sobering list, considering you thought you'd come up sevens when the publisher bought the rights to your book.

"You mean it still might not get published? Or it might be published in a way that doesn't maximize its chance of success, even in my own eyes?" you ask.

Yes. That's exactly what I mean.

Shee-yut.

And working with a major house doesn't guarantee your financial success, either. Herman Melville sold only fifty copies of *Moby-Dick* before his death. In fact, most authors with major houses never earn out their advances, meaning they never get another cent after their initial advance check. The average debut novelist with a major house, according to Gary Smailes of The Proactive Writer (http://proactivewriter.com/blog/),

7

sells about 2,000 books in the first year. If he sells 10,000 in the first year, chances are the house feels he is doing quite well. If he sells 14,000 or more in the debut year, the book will probably be deemed a big success to the house, but likely not earn the author much more than a pat on the back.

A few years ago, I stood at a crossroads in my own writing journey. I had three novels out with three great agents. I had their cell phone numbers on my iPhone. I didn't have offers of representation, but I did have phone dialogues going and requests to see rewrites. I wasn't there, but I was *this close*.

At the same time, the publishing industry was at a crossroads of its own. E-books seemed poised to take over the world. Profit margins were tight. Major authors like Stephen King (gasp, the moneymakers) were discovering self-publishing. And it wasn't just them. There were the indie authors. Amazon was offering 70% Kindle royalties. E-commerce was truly accessible, and print on demand (POD) had become almost easy. Gone were the days when a writer's only alternative to traditional publishing was an expensive vanity press. Amanda Hocking had burst onto the scene, making millions off books spurned by agents and editors. J.A. Konrath had shown that a middle-of-the-pack author could turn his backlist (backlist = all an author's books but the newest one) released from contract by his publisher and future indie-published writing into a more than respectable income.

A steady stream of authors began making their way over to Amazon. Their dribs and drabs of sales plus the sales of self-publishing rock stars summed up to something significant that the publishers felt in their wallets and in the deepest, darkest, most scared places in their hearts. The indie sales didn't, however, make much money for the self-published authors themselves, who tend to have trouble selling a copy outside of their immediate families. And 70% of nothing is, well, *nothing*. Or rather, it's nothing in terms of money, but if your goal is to share your words and your worlds, it's a whole heck of a lot of something—and to the major houses, all of that something started taking a bigger and bigger toll.

The publishers needed to figure out how all this change would impact their business model, but frankly, at the time that I was deciding whether to indie publish, they hadn't yet. Writers discovered the concept of disintermediation, where the only truly necessary players in the game of book sales were author and reader, save possibly a freelance editor, a digital artist, a publicist, and a business consultant, all of whom an author could retain for herself if she chose to.

Slim publishing-company profits narrowed further while I went back and forth over many months in dialogue with agents, and I had a decision to make: Should I keep chasing after a possibility that kept getting less likely and would cost me control of my work? I mean, who really knew what return I would get on my three novel rewrites? I certainly wasn't guaranteed representation, and even if I got it, a book sale was not an automatic. Until I signed a sales contract, the size of my potential advance would be shrinking daily, and the other terms of my deal would be growing less favorable as well, because this was business, and a business on the rocks. That potential deal would still require me to promote and market my own book on my own dime and my own time. Bottom line: I had no guarantee of a return, or even of ever traditionally publishing.

I started seriously considering throwing my hat into the ring of indie publishing. I'd still have no guarantee of a return, and I could lose my own money, at that. But the rewards were huge. I'd get the chance to share my works with whoever wanted to read it. I'd retain control—beautiful, blessed control—and publish the book of my heart, not the book of someone else's balance sheet. And that was the crux of it to me: control. I'd been an entrepreneur for nearly twenty years. I knew how to run a successful business. And promotion was a wash; I'd be doing it whether I went indie or stuck to traditional. How big a stretch was it, really, to move from entrepreneur to authorpreneur? Bottom line: I had no guarantee of a return on my investment as an indie, but I *did* have a guarantee of publishing, and I could do it my way, which is what really drove me.

You're in control

"You can make no money with someone telling you what to do, or you can make no money calling your own shots. Which one would give you more joy?" my husband asked. "And don't answer that, because I already know. So I'll help you."

And he did.

I'd love to say the result was a gusher, but I'd be lying. It was a smashing success to us, but modest by major house standards. I sold 5,000 copies of my debut novel in the first six months, and almost half of those sales were of paperbacks. Combined with Kindle giveaways during that time period, 50,000 people got a copy of *Saving Grace*. It was picked up nationwide by Hastings Entertainment for their 137 stores, and regionally by Barnes and Noble. It led to greater exposure and sales of my backlist of relationship humor books. It paved the way for my future books. It beat the performance of most debut novelists with major houses. For all of that, I am grateful and excited, but not rolling in money. What I am rich in, however, is information, tons and tons of information on indie-publishing successes and failures, good moves and missteps.

You're not alone

So here's something I know: if you indie publish, you are a needle in a haystack. In 2012 alone, 235,000 indie titles were published, representing about 43% of books published that year, according to Bowker, a company that provides bibliographic information on published works to the industry. There are more than one million Kindle e-books in publication as I type this manuscript, and that number is growing quickly. According to Penguin-owned Author Solutions (not my top choice as a service provider for indie authors, but a valid source of data), its average indie title sells 150 copies. That's not an annual number, folks, that's a forever number.

The number of competing titles is growing exponentially. Not only are individuals indie publishing, but so are businesses like *AskMen* magazine, which has launched a line of books to meet the perceived needs of its customers. And successful traditionally published authors like James Patterson are turning their brands into title-churning franchises, handing over writing duties to flocks of co-authors. So you're competing with an incredible volume of titles, traditional and indie, individual and business, and it's increasingly difficult to stand out from the crowd.

Be careful basing your "go indie" decision too heavily on widely touted indie-riches stories. For instance, *Fifty Shades of Gray* was originally indie published, but it became a massive commercial success only *after* Random House picked it up. From my perspective, it was still a huge coup that Random House discovered it.

Before you decide whether to indie publish, ask yourself:

—Can I deliver the quality needed to make sales?

—Do I have the necessary business skills?

—Can I promote my books to the point of recognition and sales?

—Will I still have time to keep writing my next books?

And, most importantly,

—Why am I choosing to indie publish?

If you only want copies of your book for yourself, your friends, and your family, and you don't care about making money, it may not matter to you if you ever sell a single book.

For some of us, despite the odds and the cons, our goals reflect our desire for independence. If you're one of those intrepid souls, stubborn to the bone and yearning to work like a pack mule, then you're just the kind of loser who's right for indie publishing.

If that's a "hell, yeah" or even a "hmmm, maybe," read on.

2 • MAKE IT LOOK EASY

Publishing is easy. Good books are hard.

There has never been a better time to be a writer. Never in the history of the world have writers so easily connected with each other and their readers. Imagine poor Jane Austen: if she wanted the feedback of a critique group, meeting them in person would have been logistically challenging and potentially socially awkward. And it would have involved writing drafts longhand and posting them in the mail. Feedback would take weeks or months.

Remember the movie *Julie and Julia*, which showed Julia Child's long and laborious process of circulating drafts and corresponding with her agent? That's hard to fathom now, with our computer-generated documents, e-mail, DropBox, Box.net, YouSendIt, and other forms of delivery ad infinitum. Traveling to conferences to learn our craft, meet agents and editors, and bond with other writers is well within our capabilities. Finding other writers (or agents, editors, digital artists, publicists, and publishers) is just a Google search away.

It gets even better. Jane Austen couldn't format her own manuscript. She didn't have the ability to Photoshop a slick cover from stock photos of English gentry and nifty Old World fonts. She couldn't submit a short-run order to a printer or order three copies of *Sense and Sensibility* online from a file she'd created. She sure as shootin' wouldn't be able to imagine an e-book, let alone create one and publish *Emma* worldwide in mere hours.

Her customers couldn't see her shortbread recipe on Pinterest, participate in her Rafflecopter giveaways, follow her gardening blog, or chat with her in her Goodreads "Tea with Jane" group. They might—and only might—find a hard copy of *Pride and Prejudice* in a big-city bookstore, years and years and years after she wrote it with a quill and ink.

We are lucky, and *spoiled.*

"Wait," I hear you say. "Did she really just call me spoiled?"

Yes, yes I did. Because I am, and you are, too. We are spoiled with this instant gratification. We expect it all to come easily, to be easy. *Really,* don't we? Compare our lives to Jane Austen's and the contrast is stark. It is so tempting to believe that writing is something that should come easily, too, and that publishing should be easy, even free. I mean, we wrote 100,000 words and tacked on "The End" and our mother told us it's better than John Irving's latest, and she ought to know, because she's in a book club. Um, yeah.

My biggest fear as I write this book is that I'll enable you to take shortcuts on your writing journey, and that you'll never make it to the ultimate destination of greatness because you took the first exit off the interstate that offered cheap gas and clean bathrooms. That would be tragic.

Yes, we have great access to writing tools, and publishing has become easier. But *becoming* a great writer takes just as many words and years as ever before. Maybe we can compress them by cutting out some of the wasted time, but you still have to put in the effort to develop your voice, your own depth, your story, and your skill in telling it. Or maybe you write nonfiction about a topic that takes many, many years to master. Those things I can't speed up for you, and I beg you not to surrender to the shiny allure of indie publishing because you believe it will be fast, cheap, or easy. Instead, turn to it because it is your business model of choice for sharing your fully mature book with the world. Or because you aspire only to share your book with close family and friends.

If you get lazy on your writing journey and succumb to premature publication, if you publish a poorly written (and/or poorly edited) book and then flog people into spending their time and money on it, heed my words: they're done with you. You'll have alienated the people you have a measure of influence over. And if you enticed unsuspecting strangers into reading schlock, you'll discover that instant gratification cuts both ways: unhappy readers can flame your book with scathing reviews online. The wrath of the Goodreads community will descend upon you. You can't delete their postings or argue them into submission (more on that later). The internet is forever, and your name is mud.

3 • WRITE IT ANYWAY

Overcoming doubts

Many of you, like me, wrestle with the question of whether you "deserve" to indie publish. Whether, after all the rejections your book baby has racked up, you should get a grip and catch a clue. Whether you have anything to say that anyone else wants or needs to hear. Whether you should just stick a three-hole-punched copy in a binder and chalk it up to an experimental phase in your life. I can't answer those questions for you any more than I can answer them for me.

I am a huge advocate, though, of delaying gratification until you are as sure as you can ever be that your book is ready, mostly through validation by credible outside sources. Obviously, I've clicked the metaphorical publishing button many times now. Is it because I am convinced that my books rock, and I have no doubts left to torment me? Unfortunately, no. I'm just as tormented as any other writer.

So wrestle a few doubts with me as we move to the inevitable conclusion: we're gonna write it anyway, so why not indie publish?

On being a writer

Every time I publish a book, I imagine snide comments from unseen naysayers: "So where do you get off, calling yourself a writer? You've never been traditionally published."

Not to get snippy about it, but I am traditionally published, just not in fiction and not as a solo writer. I co-authored a nonfiction tome-o-excitement that the former Prentice Hall published ten years ago, and I have had a slew of nonfiction articles published over the years.

But is it only traditionally published writing that makes one a writer? Or publication at all, in any form, for that matter? Because I believe I was a writer long before any of my books came out, traditionally or indie published.

I am a writer. I write because it's in my DNA. It's what I do, how I express myself, how I make my living. In my day job as a workplace investigator, I crank out a couple of 5,000-word reports each month for an hourly fee—a large hourly fee, which technically makes me a paid writer. It's far more lucrative than I ever expect my published writing to be, which begs the question, I know, of why I'd waste my time on indie publishing.

How about teaching? Does that factor in? I taught writing to wannabe lawyers at the University of Texas School of Law. But it was legal writing, and trust me, legal writing is boring and repetitive . . . and did I mention it's boring and repetitive?

I've written a lot of books. About half a million words published, and another 250,000 waiting in the wings. I'll write many more before I'm through. And even that is not enough. I blog, for my own site and two others, which accounts for another couple thousand words per week. For goodness' sake, the volume of my Facebook status updates alone qualifies me as a writer. I can't help it. Addiction is a disability, for real.

I call myself a writer, not because of any of that, but because deep down, where hope incubates belief, I am a writer. It is a matter of identity. It's not that I am a writer of narrative nonfiction or business publications or harassment-investigation reports or even mysterious fiction.

I am simply a writer.

When I need to explain myself, I turn to writing. When I want to share my feelings, I write them down. I courted my husband with my written words while he wooed me with his spoken ones. I hate the telephone—I want to put it in writing. Sure, I'll take a meeting, but expect to hear from me in writing afterward.

My writing even wins awards, for reasons I don't understand. My mother always told me that being a giant smart-ass wouldn't pay off. I guess we know who got the last laugh on that one. People buy my books, they write term papers on them, they write letters to me about them, and some even send me gifts. (Keep it coming, people.)

But was it any of these awesome things—these validations— that tipped the scales for me from non-writer to writer?

Negatory. No one has to bless my writing to deem me a writer.

I breathe. I walk and talk. I eat, I sleep. I write. And I won't let anyone tell me any different.

Will you?

On the dreaded urge to quit

People accuse me of perkiness—usually people who know me only at arm's length. And those who forget I am forty-something-something years old. Perkiness is a youthful thing, if you ask me.

Those who know me well call me more-accurate and less-flattering names. I'm "a challenge," a tiger, the General, overly dramatic, moody, emotional, a hormonal werewolf. I am driven, goal-oriented, type A, and a little OCD. My closest peeps know that I am reclusive and borderline antisocial, and at the same time well honed in groups and public speaking. I wouldn't go so far as to say I'm agoraphobic, but I hate to venture out of my house unless it's with my husband. When he's not around, I can go days on end in my pink flannel sleepy sheep PJs without leaving the sanctuary of my carefully arranged tower of pillows that form the chair back to the chair bottom provided by my mattress.

All of these things, yes.

No one describes me as querulous. Yet, as I click these keys, querulous I undoubtedly am.

Today, I am full of self-doubt.

Today I want to quit trying to be a writer.

If I were to indulge this mood, I'd rip all my books from the shelves of every bookstore and burn them. I'd close down my website. I'd crawl back into the cave I emerged from when I warbled out in a twangy voice that cracked on the third word, "I'm a writer, y'all."

I honestly do not know if I have what it takes to do this well. I look at what I have produced so far, and I don't know. I don't know I don't know I don't know. I can't see the forest for the trees, the leaves, the stems, the bark. I can't see squat. My fears could crush my heart like a stinkbug under a boot heel.

I am querulous. Whiny. Peevish. Fretful. I'd add to that unappreciative, since I know, relatively speaking, how much success I've enjoyed in this short time. Yep, I admit it. Ungrateful. Lacking in appreciation for my blessings.

I am usually the positive one who cheers myself and everyone else on, but days like this are dark. I know I'll return to myself eventually. Soon, even. In the meantime, it's time for a hot soak and a book deserving of the trees that died to make it. Because who am I kidding? I could no more stop writing than I could cut my index fingers off with a butter knife.

On perseverance

I've written four novels, filled reams of paper with business writing, and killed a forest with narrative nonfiction. I don't pretend I am a great writer. I'm becoming whatever writer it is I have the potential to be.

Ten years after first dipping my toe into fiction, I don't know whether I am a decent fledgling novelist or not. I do know this: I am fifty bajillion times better than when I started. And I won't fulfill my potential—however modest—unless I keep writing. I may write ten novels before the potential gels. I dunno. I do know that if I stop, it will stagnate.

I have to write to be a writer.

Every time I sit down to write, I feel another piece of the puzzle fall into place. Maybe I finally understand how to rewrite my way out of a problem whose solution has eluded me for three years. Maybe I make my novel better. Tighter. Tenser. Faster. Let's say it's the best I have done so far. That it's the best I was capable of as of yesterday.

It is not the best I will ever do, or better than what I will write today.

Because three years and three more books from now, I will have grown. Every single time I feel like quitting because it's so *hard* and it isn't happening fast enough for me, I will have a cry and try again. On days when a story has me by the throat and I have to work my day job, I will rise at 3:00 a.m., make coffee, and write.

Practice makes perfect.

Here's the unvarnished truth: I have no idea on any day whether what I write will suck. I can edit it tomorrow and it may still suck. It may always suck. C'est la vie.

It will still be worth every second I invested in it. It will be forevermore a part of my becoming.

So I will tilt my chin toward the sun and, just for today, I will believe. I may publish my work in progress. I may not. But if nothing else, I will continue to write it, and the next "it," too.

4 • NAIL IT DOWN

Clearing up (some of) the confusion amongst and between traditional publishing, indie publishing, self-publishing, and hybrid publishing

OK, so by now hopefully we can all agree that way back when dinosaurs roamed the earth, an author's publishing choices were limited to traditional presses and the so-called vanity presses. Vanity presses got their name because they were so expensive that only authors with the money to indulge their vanity could afford to print their books, which they usually ended up giving away or storing in a shrine.

E-commerce, e-books, and POD have *nearly* relegated vanity press to a historical phenomenon. Today, authors can independently publish books of any degree of quality or lack thereof in a much more affordable fashion. Certainly, that enables some authors to misguidedly—through ignorance or, yes, even the dreaded vanity—publish works that maybe should have stayed hidden on a hard drive somewhere. It also, as discussed in chapter 1, partly levels the playing field, allowing talented writers to retain control and take charge of their writing careers.

The complexity of the decision tree on how to publish makes graphic designers shiver in horror. Here is my highly simplified view of the choices:

The traditional model

With the assistance of an agent, an author sells a manuscript to one of the Big Four publishing houses (or their many subsidiaries): Hachette Book Group, HarperCollins, Simon & Schuster, and Penguin Random House. The house usually pays a monetary advance to the author, and the author always gives away a percentage of royalties to the agent and to the house to cover their investments and potential profits. The size of the advance and the percentages vary, but the author does not generally pay anything up front. The contract may grant the publisher rights to the author's next several books or right of first refusal on the next one. It also determines which formats the manuscript will be published in and which bookstores it will be marketed to, and often allows a year of lead time before publication. The house distributes the book through its networks as best it can. At some point, the house may relinquish rights back to the author, although this has become increasingly complex with the advent of e-books. I'll call this model the major house throughout *Loser*.

The small-to-medium-sized press model

Still traditional, but not one of the major houses. With or without the assistance of an agent, an author sells a manuscript to a small-to-medium-sized press—many of which define themselves as indies, since they are independent of the major houses. Sometimes the house pays a modest monetary advance to the author, and the author always gives a percentage of the royalties to the agent (if there was one) and to the house to cover its investments and potential profits. Percentages vary. The author often does not pay anything up front. Sometimes the author contracts for several books or for right of first refusal for the publisher on a next book. The house publishes the manuscript in the formats it deems prudent and markets it to the appropriate booksellers, as specified in the contract, but normally with a smaller budget than a major house. There is usually a year or more of lead time before the house distributes as best it can through its networks, which generally are smaller than those of a major house. At some point, the house may relinquish publication rights to the author, although this issue has become increasingly complex with the advent of e-books. You'll see me refer to this model as small press. Some small presses classify themselves as indie because they are independent of the Big Four; I won't argue with that. A rose by any other name, you know? They're just not as independent as the author who goes it alone.

The indie or self-published models

Pure Indie, Maverick

An author performs or procures the services of the providers needed to independently publish a manuscript under his own name or a name he creates for his indie-publishing venture. Some authors secure all these services under one umbrella, like through CreateSpace. Others work with individual providers for each service, like I do. The author covers all of his own costs. The author chooses the formats to publish, the timeline, and the distribution channels to pursue.

Note: Authors whose traditional publishers have released their rights can republish their books independently without investing in the manuscript consultation and editing that a first-time indie-published author should undergo. Authors like J.A. Konrath and Dean Wesley Smith have been quite successful on this path. They both have very informative blogs, which I cite in the appendices. I suggest you do some serious reading on their sites. You won't regret it.

Author-Assisted

An author contracts with an author-assistance company that bundles the services needed to independently publish the manuscript, either under the company's name or a name the author chooses. The author covers all of his own costs through payment to the service company, a royalty, or some combination of the two. The author's choices about which formats to publish, the timeline, and the distribution channels to pursue are limited by the company and its contract.

This model should be called "author, assisted," but I call it "author-assisted" without the comma because I pay my editor by the word, and anything I can do to lose those six characters saves me a couple of cents. Damn, that sentence just ate up all my savings.

Indie-to-Traditional, Hybrid

An author publishes independently, then gains notice from traditional publishing houses. The author contracts with a publisher (major house or small press), with or without an agent, and follows some or all of the traditional model. Texas author Rhiannon Frater went hybrid when she successfully moved a zombie trilogy from indie to Tor Publishing. Hugh Howey went hybrid when he kept e-book rights to his originally indie-published sci-fi *Wool* but contracted the print rights to Simon & Schuster.

Basic features of indie-publishing options

Endless variations flow from each indie-publishing model, but they have several factors in common. First, in each one, the author bears primary responsibility for promoting and marketing his own book. Second, the author always bears the cost for the book to be published, whether through royalty shares, direct payment to a press or author-service company, payments to various individual service providers, or some combination thereof.

The challenge for indie authors is to find a simple business model that doesn't leave them vulnerable to an author-service company that paints an unrealistic sales picture and demands exorbitant fees and/or royalty splits. Because, remember, the average author who publishes with Penguin's Author Solutions sells 150 books. The definition of average here is "most of us." Please bear that in mind and factor it into what you spend.

How easy can it get?

The easiest model for a pure indie craving simplicity is to publish POD through Amazon's CreateSpace and e-books through Amazon's Kindle Direct Publishing (KDP). Later chapters will discuss CreateSpace and KDP at length. CreateSpace offers all the services an author needs to bring a book to market, but it has drawbacks; it may not provide the best services or the best price, and it requires the author to give up some distribution possibilities. I'll flesh this choice out further when we get to the discussion of strategy.

If an author is willing to accept a more complex business model in order to retain choices, maximize quality, and minimize cost, then we've got a lot to talk about.

5 • JOIN THE COOL KIDS' CLUB

Losers are the new cool kids. If you weren't already convinced that this indie thing is for you, hold on to your taters. Literary snobs need not apply!

PART TWO:
SOCIAL CLIMBING FOR SUBVERSIVES

This is the moment when you should reread the part in the introduction about why you should not skip parts 2 and 3, but if you're convinced that you need express-lane access to publication and can't slow down to read that which could literally save your career, don't blame me later. Now, do what you're gonna do, and I'll see you wherever you land.

6 • MIND YOUR OWN BUSINESS

Learn all you can about the indie-publishing business.

Once upon a time, you probably didn't know how to do something, or at least didn't know how to do it very well. If not, pretend for me. And see the note above on vanity presses.

What do we do when we don't know how to do something well—take for instance indie publishing? We seek knowledge, like you're doing with Loser. We attend workshops, like people do who come to my Loser classes. If you can't come to mine, chances are your nearest writers' group sponsors similar ones. You can also take webinars and college courses.

Let me throw it out there that while you're learning about indie publishing, maybe even while you're indie publishing, you'd be well-served to treat writing like something you don't know how to do well enough. I don't mean to hurt your feelings, but writing is something we should strive to improve every day for the rest of our lives, even after we've published one book, ten books, or one hundred books. So read books on your craft, read the works of writers you admire in your genre or field, read the works of writers you don't admire, and read outside your genre, too, every now and then. Attend writers conferences, retreats, and workshops. Maybe even get your masters in fine arts (there are online programs available these days, such as University of Texas at El Paso (http://academics.utep.edu/Default.aspx?tabid=42392) or apply for a prestigious immersive program or fellowship. I mean, why not? The worst that could happen is you win the Nobel Prize in Literature or something.

The main thing is this: don't get in a rush. If you rush, it shows, and I already talked in chapter 2 about the perils of sucking publicly. I don't recommend it. If your ideas or expertise took you twenty years to develop, what's twenty months or twenty weeks more to polish them to a brilliant shine?

7 • FIND STRENGTH IN SUBMISSION

Ways to make money as a writer before you indie publish

Inevitably, the process of writing and publishing your book takes time. Monetizing that effort is not an overnight event, either. Wouldn't it be nice to establish your writing creds, improve your writing, and possibly make a little cash in the meantime? The nice thing is that anything you do to get your name out there, whether before or after you indie publish, will ultimately help you sell books. Even publication of excerpts or adaptations of your book will work. That, my friends, is called multipurposing. I love multipurposing.

Here are some ideas for what to write during your downtime:

Greeting cards

Want to write one-liners, poems, and narratives for greeting cards? It's surprisingly lucrative. Blue Mountain Arts (http://www.sps.com/help/writers_guidelines.html), for example, pays $300 for each accepted submission. I have a friend who made thousands writing greeting cards before she published her novels. Just type in a web search of "greeting card writer submissions" and watch the opportunities gush forth.

Freelance articles

You can submit short works of fiction and nonfiction to online and print periodicals fairly easily, and most publications post their submission guidelines online. I published a short piece for parents of ADHD kids in *ADDitude Magazine* (http://www.additudemag.com/adhd/writers-guidelines.html) a while ago, and although they don't post their pay rates online, I will say that I was happy with what they paid me. And they allowed me to repurpose content from my indie-published book *The Clark Kent Chronicles* and give credit to our publishing company, SkipJack Publishing.

Ah, that magical word of shimmery awesomeness: REPURPOSE. I highly recommend as much of that as possible.

Anthologies

Here's a space where I've gotten very lucky. When my local writers' group, the Houston Writers Guild, put out a call for submissions for *Ghosts* a few years ago, I repurposed an excerpt from one of my upcoming novels. That worked so well that I answered another call, and I'd soon placed repurposed pieces from another novel and two nonfiction books in *OMG—That Woman!* Around that same time, a website I wrote for hooked me into two other anthologies. None of these publications paid me, but I did get free copies of the books, and better yet, I got my name and work out there. What's to stop you from putting together an anthology yourself, if you can't find one? I'll share more below on searching out submission calls.

Local periodicals

You know how Jan Karon got her start on her beloved Mitford novels? Writing a column for a local newspaper called *The Blowing Rocket* in Blowing Rock, North Carolina. Why not contact periodicals in your area and try your hand at building a local readership?

Short stories

Here's a fun one for writers fifty and older: HuffPost50 (http://www.huffingtonpost.com/2013/04/24/huffpost50-fiction-seeking-short-stories_n_3141218.html). Or if you want to aim higher, try Glimmer Train (http://www.glimmertrain.com/writguid1.html). If you type in a search for "fiction short story submissions"—or nonfiction—you'll unearth some gems.

Other calls for submissions

Calls for submissions go out every day; the question is how to find them. Two great places to start are *Poets & Writers* (http://www.pw.org/classifieds) and Writer's Relief (http://client.writersrelief.com/writers-classifieds/anthology-calls-for-submissions.aspx). Or just get to Googling.

8 • RUIN YOUR REPUTATION

Set your publishing goals and accept that most of them require promotion and visibility.

Most writers accept that with publication comes visibility. But what most of them don't understand is that not *much* visibility comes without promotion. And most writers won't take the steps necessary for that promotion, and then they're shocked when their sales don't meet expectations. Then they complain about it at length, bemoaning the death of the "pure writer" who didn't get her hands dirty with all that nastiness. Puh-leeze.

Woopsie. I almost climbed up on my favorite soapbox. I'll save it for later. Let's back up a step.

Why'd you write a book in the first place, anyway?

It's time to talk turkey: what *are* your goals for your books? Here are some valid options:

1. Write 50,000 words and finish with "The End"

2. See your book in print

3. Give copies to your family and friends

4. Build it and hope someone comes (publication without promotion)

5. Market your nonfiction book in conjunction with your professional services

6. Sell as many copies as you can within your time and budget constraints

7. Go all in and settle for nothing less than literary domination

What do you want out of publishing?

All of your choices in indie publishing should stem from your goals. Some goals have the potential to lead to visibility. Others don't. If all you want is the warm, gooey satisfaction of reaching "The End" and seeing a print copy with a glossy cover in your own private library, then no one ever has to know you're a writer. You don't have to worry about crass promotion or nerve-racking public appearances.

You'll still need to know how to get from "once upon a time" to "print on demand," though. All of the others will require varying degrees of promotion, so remaining a secret is actually a bad thing. If number seven is your goal, then I hope you are a trust-fund baby or have a spouse who provides all the income your family needs (plus a lot of cash for you to invest in your books), because you will not only have to write fantastic books, but you will need to invest serious time and money into promoting them. Even if you commit to it full time, odds are you won't be the next Janet Evanovich. But if you're having fun and eventually eke out a living, do you even care? Just keep on keeping on.

Should you use your real name?

If it really wigs you out to think that strangers know your name and may stalk you at the Piggly Wiggly, then you are clearly delusional can always use a pseudonym. While there are valid reasons to use a pen name, like when you write kids' books and erotica and don't want a Google search to pull up your picture books alongside your secret smutty gems, the downside is that most writers can barely sell their books to their families, which they count on for the grassroots referrals that will build their audience. If even the author's family can't find her book on Amazon—because one should never underestimate just how hard most people can make the process—then she has hit a serious stumbling block. Personally, I want to capitalize on any recognition I can get from my personal and professional life bleeding over into my writing life. If, despite me waving the caution flag, you decide to use a pseudonym, please for the love of Pete only use one. If and when you finally gain some sales traction and name recognition with your ultimate audience, you shouldn't start over.

Who are your target readers?

Goal-setting helps you clarify your audience. If the audience is yourself, or even just friends and family, you may not care about investing in quality production at the same level as you would for the public. If the audience is the public, you will have to consider a more serious investment. I'll address what kinds of investments soon.

9 • PLAN YOUR ATTACK

Indie publishing is a business and it requires a good business plan.

Once you're clear about your goals, it's time to figure out how to achieve them. Don't roll your eyes at me, now. Buck up and put on your big-girl panties: writing is an art, but publishing is a business. Would you invest your time and money in someone else's business if they didn't have a good business plan? Well, why invest it in your own, then???

Setting the right goals ensures that you put the right elements into your plan and that you don't waste time on things that won't move you toward your goals. If you don't want to market your book, for instance, you won't waste time on social media and can maintain a sense of disdain for us lollabouts that do.

If you've never written a business plan, there's no time like the present to start, and I'm here to help. Below is a basic outline. Maybe following this structure will jump-start your inner business engine. It's not rocket science. It's mostly just getting organized and realistic about how your business will work, and committing that to writing. If you want to see a good example, visit D. D. Scott's website *The Writer's Guide to E-Publishing* and read the three-part series by Denise Grover Swank called "A Business Plan for Self-Published Authors" (http://thewritersguidetoepublishing.com/a-business-plan-for-self-published-authors-part-one-of-a-three-part-series). While her outline does not follow mine below *exactly*, it's pretty darn close, and her analysis of her growing business and evolving strategy is honest and helpful.

The elements of a business plan

1. Mission statement and goals

2. Description of business

3. Ownership and location of business

4. Products

5. Market analysis

6. Strategy and implementation

7. Pricing plan

8. Financial plan

9. Timeline

10. Marketing plan (and here I believe you need a separate plan unto itself for each book)

11. Summary

Just as soon as you write this outline, it becomes clear that not only do you need goals, but you also need strategy. In order to make strategic decisions, we need to explore a few topics in more detail. Fear not. By the time you finish reading *Loser*, you'll have learned enough strategy and how to execute it to draft your first indie-publishing business plan, complete with estimated cost and a rough timeline (with a 20% inflator, because life happens).

Sweet.

Make a writing plan, too.

It's soooo easy to stop writing. Writing is hard. Writing hurts. Writing is time consuming. Writing doesn't love you back. But if you want to indie publish successfully, you need volume, you need a backlist, you need complementary titles. You need to keep writing. So set up an editorial calendar for your planned books. You can always change the plan, but without a plan, it is hard to have an editorial calendar. Then create a daily schedule that includes time to write. If you fall behind, schedule a makeup weekend and write your hands off until you catch up. Or don't. It's up to you. But if you're thinking, "I want to be a multi-title author, I want to have a backlist, I want to be prolific," you'll have to work hard and employ a lot of self-discipline to get there. No fairy dust or magic beans will do the trick.

Are you working on your first book now? Well, you won't publish it a week after you reach "The End." Or you shouldn't, anyway. You need time to rewrite it ad nauseum, time for a critique group to help you improve it, time for a manuscript consult with a story specialist—sometimes time for several of these—and, finally, time for a comprehensive edit followed by beta reads. Otherwise, you run the risk of publishing toilet paper. Meanwhile, you write the next one.

Part of your timeline necessarily includes writing your books. Note that I said *books* plural, not *book* singular. Why? Because no matter which publishing model you adopt, rare is the author who makes a living with one book. If earning an income is not your goal, write as few books as you want. No problem. But if you want to make money, plan on a minimum of four complementary books whose sales build upon each other and in which you can concentrate a single, comprehensive marketing strategy.

OK, confession: I am a multiple-personality-disordered author. Of my first six books, not one of them was in the same genre. Complementariness (yeah, that's not a word, I know) rating on a scale of one to ten? About a two. But my plan included books in the same genre, and I have since stuck to my plan. Plus, I have an excuse: I'd already written all the books, so it seemed a shame not to give them each their day. I found that, while they did not cross-pollinate each other in sales in stores and online, being a multi-title author still helped me immensely. When I appear at events, the people who come usually buy more than one of my books (and sometimes all of them). This helps make my events much more profitable. It also impresses the bookstore management. Beyond making me money, my multiple titles give me credibility.

So don't fear publishing noncomplementary books. Just know that financial success most likely only comes after you have several books working together to maximize your penetration of one market segment. And that you have to write them in order to have them to publish. Same thing with complementary books. To be a financially successful indie author, you will need to be *somewhat* prolific.

Is it just me, or does "prolific" sound like the kind of thing you might catch from a public toilet? Well, whatever it is, I don't have *that*. I do, however, have a fairly strong work ethic, thanks to my father. Any time we goofed around when we should have been working, he would admonish us, "Don't just stand there playing with yourself." Yes, my mom loved this just as much as my brother and I did. Especially when he hollered it out to us on the basketball court or baseball field, with all the other (normal) parents around.

With his words of wisdom resounding in my head, I published my first six books in 2012 (other than my multi-author efforts, which I'm not counting here). I will publish two more in 2013, and two more in 2014. I plan to keep writing and publishing.

There are no magical powers involved. My plan is simple: when I finish one book, I don't stand there playing with myself (!), I start another. Maybe I take a short break to rejuvenate my brain, but I keep it short and stick to a schedule. And then I write.

Sure, you're thinking, *so do I*. Many of you do. I learned from some of you.

Some of you don't. (Although I am not suggesting that you're standing there, well, *you know*.)

When I say I start another book, I mean that I do not wait to see what happens with the current book. I mean I write "The End" and I start the next one. Now, I only devote three to four hours a day to writing (which includes books, blogs, business reports, and other schlock), because I'm not a superhero, but I play one on TV. That leaves me time to decide what to do with the last book I've finished, and to hand it off to the critiquers or the editor or for formatting, depending on what stage it's in. It leaves some time for the business of publishing, promotion, mothering, wife-ing, working out, and a part-time day job. Just not a lot of time, so, even though I'm pretty darn quick and I prioritize and time-manage down to the minute, not everything gets taken care of every day. My house is a disaster. So is my hair. I rarely cook, I don't watch much TV, and I have no social life beyond my husband and kids. In short, I'm a hot mess, but it works for me.

My advice is simple, take it or leave it: Don't just stand there playing with yourself. Make a plan and keep writing. The end.

10 • PUT IT ALL OUT THERE

How to get comfortable with visibility

As you write your Great American Novel or memoir or how-to book, most of you do it in seclusion. But publishing is public. If you publish in seclusion, your sales will be quite dismal. Thus, a solitary writer needs to work up the courage to put it out there long before the day comes that your tome blazes into glory.

And one of the hardest things about writing, any writing, is putting it out there. I'll bet you can remember the first time you put your heart on paper and let someone else see you bleed. Scary stuff, isn't it? Whether it's a paper in college, a blog post, a short story for a contest, or sometimes even a Facebook post, it's scary. Been there. Hurt like that.

I've spent my whole life pretending I was a writer that wasn't a *writer*. In fact, I spent most of my life pretending I was things I wasn't or didn't want to be, things that satisfied what I thought people expected of me. Things that made me serious. Successful. Safe. I played to my weaknesses, because then I could protect my strengths from exposure, keep them whole, keep myself whole. Maybe this makes sense to some of you. Maybe you've been there and hurt like that.

I chose a career where I had to write, but it was only words, not *words*. I entered a world of other people's stories, not my own. I spent twenty years at it. I'm still doing it, in fact. I did the same thing in my personal life. With my first marriage. With athletics. With music. I put on a mask and played pretend.

Until a few years ago, when I found my courage. I used it to try out my voice. It wasn't much of a voice, but the only way it was going to get stronger, better, truer, was if I kept using it.

So that's what I did. I spent four years training, learning, practicing, growing, strengthening. I listened to other voices. I sang along with them at times. Other times, I took the harmony role or struck out on a melody all my own. Over four years, my voice sang one million words through my fingers. One million words. That's five million letters, spaces, commas, periods, and God knows what else. It's five hundred blog posts on innumerable websites. It's songs, poems, short stories, and essays. It's five award-winning narrative nonfiction books and four novels, themselves the winners of multiple awards.

It sounds good, but a lot of it was crap, or at least started as crap. That's why it took four years. Hell, I can write fifteen hundred words an hour in my sleep. I could have done the million in that first year and called it a wrap. I didn't just write those one million words, I rewrote them, over and over and over.

There were five clear points along the way where I had to overcome an absolute maelstrom of doubt and fear inside me, but when I did, when I did *it*—put it out there—it moved me forward exponentially. These five points were the reason for those one million words; not just the words as I first wrote them, but the words they became. As one writer to another, I want to share these points with you in case they help you put it out there, too. They were essential to my journey. You know the one: the writer's journey. The one you're on, if you're reading this book.

The first—hitting Publish on my first blog. Sounds goofy now when I say it, but I thought I would turn to stone when I clicked the Publish button the first time. It got me over the fear that others would hear *me* and not like me. Worse, that they would tell me so.

The second? Letting an editor read my work, a big-time editor. That was scary like the thought of ever using an Epilady again. The conversation I had with that editor was one of the most important in my writing life. She gave me hope without promises. Reality. It was twenty minutes of her life, and it was the next forty years of mine. Thank you, Jane Friedman.

The third was writing about the subjects most painful and personal to me in the first person and getting the hell over it being about me. Alcoholism. My flaws as a parent. The challenges I face in personal relationships. I learned to access those emotions, those humiliations, doubts, and pains, and put them out there, and *separate myself* from them. Bonus: this evolved into narrative nonfiction books that I am told help other people. That motivates me. I eventually channeled that into strangers, into fiction.

The fourth: when an agent read my whole manuscript. Read two of my whole manuscripts, in fact, back to back. I got the best advice of my fledgling writing career from her: Writing *is* rewriting, and voice without fully realized craft is not enough. Thank you, Elizabeth Pomada. I took it to heart and spent the next two years working on craft. It paid off.

And the fifth? Entering my books in contests to be judged, scored, rated, compared, and critiqued. Thank you, writers, editors, and agents who give their time to make this possible for all of us.

Putting it out there. It's what propels me forward on the path, sometimes in small steps and sometimes in quantum leaps. And it never stops, never, ever, ever stops. One million public words. That's putting it out there. And if I want to make this writer's gig my career, to make money by indie publishing, I have to continue putting it out there. So, world, here's my heart, you hold it in your hands. Take my soul, pass it around. You have my blessing.

11 • PRACTICE COMPULSIVELY

On the practice of writing and establishing a writing practice

As my cover proclaims, my name is Pamela Fagan Hutchins. Guess what my fabulous editor, Meghan Pinson, calls me? Pamela Friggin' Hutchins. She swears she means it as a compliment, but I'm not sure she always uses it that way. She's talking at least some of the time about my self-discipline and the volume of words I write. In other words, I practice my writing, and I have established a writing practice.

Huh?

The writing practice, y'all. Surely you've heard the term? It's about establishing a methodology and a rhythm that works for you, that keeps you going on that ambitious four-complementary-books-plus business plan you're starting to put together. It's about doing it instead of just thinking about it or talking about it.

Ahhhhh . . . yes, the practice of writing. It's a structure that helps you become more practiced, more polished, more skilled in your writing.

As I sit here writing *Loser*, guess how many of my novels were drafted originally during the annual National Novel Writing Month (NaNoWriMo)?

** THREE **

That's right—I gave birth to three Sagittarians, then nurtured them in the ensuing months as lovingly as I would a human baby. That got them to the point of crappy-first-draft status. From there, many more months and much hard work later, I had something I could turn over to my editor.

NaNoWriMo works for me.

It works for some other folks, too. It does not work AT ALL for a great number of people.

First, let me explain. NaNoWriMo takes place over thirty days each year during November. During NaNoWriMo, participants are challenged to write a 50,000-word "novel." They are urged to curb their inner editor and bear down until they reach the word-count goal. They are not tasked to write good fiction. They are not even required to reach "The End." In fact, you could type your name in, copy, paste, and repeat until you hit 50,000 words, and they would never know. But *you* would, so don't do it because you'd hate yourself for it.

So why do people do it? For me, it was a cattle prod to the haunches. I flourish under deadlines and pressure. I sit on my tush and eat bonbons the rest of the time. OK, that's not true. But I do have a lot of competing priorities, and I need a reason to put writing at the top of the list. For people like me, it provides just the right structure and conditions to make us work on our writing. Not necessarily work well, but work.

For others, NaNoWriMo is a spirit-crushing venture doomed for failure. These are the folks who can work steadily at a middlin' pace day after day, but who absolutely freeze, creatively or otherwise, with the clock ticking. NaNoWriMo for them is cruel and unusual punishment at best, and, at worst, crippling.

Thus, before you sign up for NaNoWriMo, decide which team you play on, Team Adrenaline or Team Consistency. If you're an adrenaline junkie like me, the next decision point is preparedness.

I highly advocate completion of a full outline and/or a synopsis before November first, otherwise you may spend the rest of your life deciphering the hidden meaning in your speed writing. Actually, for me, writing an outline or a synopsis is a must before I start any book.

Next, figure out whether you will be able to clear your decks to ensure success. The pace is only 1,700 words per day, but life has a way of stealing writing days. My max day during NaNoWriMo was 10,000 words, a feat I pulled off because I "had to," due to lost writing days. I had to wrap my hands in ice packs and elevate them for hours afterwards. Put off the deadline on anything else you can. Line up your support team. Who's going to feed the kids and pets? Pay the bills? Take out the garbage? Prepare your family mentally and run NaNo drills to ready them.

Lastly, remind yourself going in that at best you will end up with a too-short-for-prime-time novel in shitty-first-draft shape. Too many novice writers think that reaching the end of NaNoWriMo means you have a work worthy of pushing out to readers everywhere. Um, you probably don't. Be patient. Work it, rework it, and re-rework it some more. You'll get there (probably), but writing must cure before consumption. My NaNoWriMo from year one was published five years later. I can't count the rewrites, but writing IS rewriting. Really, it is.

For me, creativity follows productivity. Sure, inspiration randomly strikes at times, but not often. Mostly, I buckle down and, by pushing myself through the process, jump-start my creative mind. It's more like deliberate creativity, and it works. As the word count grows, my brain has more to work with.

Write now. Rewrite later.

Can't wait for November? Start the clock on thirty days, set aside a few hours a day to write, and budget your words for each day. Then start on page one and don't turn back until you hit your goals. It's a fantastic way to get a first draft.

If you can't work at that pace, then extend your timeline but follow the same process. The idea is to work forward along a linear path. To establish a practice that with input (your time and your words) leads to output (books, baby, books). To write with purpose.

Write it your way.

Some people are cursing me right now because they feel that sort of schedule messes with their art. Well, they aren't usually the people who are making a decent living as writers. There, I said it. And now they all hate me, and the three exceptions to this rule are going to light my inbox on fire. That's fine. I can take it. If my advice helps the rest of you establish your practice, then it's well worth it.

A practice. For some of you, this means you write at the same time every day. I do. From one to five p.m.—unless I have professional or familial obligations to contend with, in which case I get up at the ass crack of predawn and slodge it out then. And when I'm on deadline, I extend my hours into the evening. When I'm behind schedule, I write around the clock. But mostly I write in the afternoon. Since I usually have several diverse writing projects going on at once, I try to block off chunks of time for each so I can sustain concentration.

Many people have a particular place they write best. I like to mix it up, but I have a work-from-home husband, three offspring at home, four dogs, and a duck. (Yes, a duck.) That means hibernation, so I prop myself onto pillows in my bedroom. On the blessed days that the house is empty of other humans, my laptop and I move my big black comfy office chair around the house at our whim. I find changing locations energizes my brain. For this reason, I love to do rewrites on vacations. And I love most of all to write when I'm in the country, like at our sixteen acres in the middle of Nowheresville, Texas. Do what works for you.

More important than place to me, though, is that I have all my stuff. I need a yellow pad and a pen, my laptop du jour, a scrunchie and a headband, and snacks and drinks within reach. Oh, and allergy meds. My iPhone. My Boston terrier. And silence. No music, please.

Your stuff will be your own, but gather it before you sit down to write so you won't have excuses to keep getting up to fetch things.

The key to your writing practice is finding the elements that, when put together, stimulate your productivity and creativity. Your hours, your place, your stuff. Figure them out, then commit to yourself to stick to it. Commit before witnesses in writing so you won't fall off your practice in a few months. Or hours.

And that brings us to the subject of writer's block.

When the muse is fickle

Sometimes my fingers fly and I still can't keep up with the words pouring out of my head and across the screen. Literally, the characters dance ahead of me across the lines, turning, stopping, taunting, tongues out and thumbs in ears with fingers waggling, the little scoundrels.

Other times, my fingers hover uneasily, waiting for divine inspiration, guilty with inactivity, searching for something to deliver—if not to the screen, then to my stomach in compensation. Maybe if we feed the muse, she will deliver unto us again?

She doesn't, but my butt grows bigger in my cushy black office chair, the one I bought at a yard sale for $25, the most comfortable chair I've ever owned. But that's off topic. A bigger butt? Not the desired outcome.

One month, I wrote 70,000 words. Three months later, I submitted a completed novel based on those words to my editor. It was beautiful, it was the best thing I'd ever written.

"Holy crap," I thought. "I've figured this writing thing out. I can DO this."

I sat down again in mid-July. I flexed my fingers. I wiggled them, waggled them. I placed them on the keys.

Nothing.

I adjusted my position in my seat. A few pages of wooden, colorless gibberish spurted out like literary baby poo.

I ate some slutty brownies. I repositioned my tush in its throne, the seat a bit tighter now, but for a good cause. I ground through 20,000 words of garbage over the next three weeks. I cried. I cried some more. I bought new running shoes. I went out to run and came back inside. I was too fat to run in 100 degrees.

What. The. Hell??

By August first, I was in a panic. My rough manuscript was due September first. I begged for an extension. I got two weeks. Meanwhile, real life caught up with me, ate up my window of writing opportunity. A visit from the mother-in-law for a few weeks. Kids home for the summer. The day job rearing its ugly head after a blessed break.

All of this overtook me and left me high and dry, *until* I thought I left my laptop cord at my parents' house. Now, it turns out I didn't actually leave it there. Hold that thought. But the *belief* that it was missing was critical. Because I'd bought a new laptop at the beginning of July. A different laptop than the piece-o-crap that I typed my last 6.5 books on. *That* laptop got fried by an aftermarket power cord early in its life, and even the greatness that is MicroCenter could not restore it to its original awesomeness. I suffered through with it for far too long after that ugly incident. It also has a piece of duct tape where a key I have learned to live without used to be. It looks pretty classy. Cheap-ass that I am (thanks, Dad, I got all my best qualities from you), I refused to give in. I soldiered on through problems interminable for another year with that thing. Then, after I wrote "The End" on *Saving Grace* and sent it to Meghan, I bought the shiny new machine I'd been using for this new manuscript.

Oh, it's beautiful. It is sooooo much easier to use than the old one. It has a name: the Zenbook. Peace flows like a river from its keys. So happy was I about the new possibilities of the Zenbook that I rented an office, to create further peace in my world. The office was quiet. Cool. Dark, like I crave, vampire that I am. The Zenbook and I should have been HEROIC under those conditions.

Should.

Should have been.

Alas, we did not live up to expectations.

And then . . . then . . . then, I thought I lost my Zenbook power cord. For three angst-ridden hours, I was forced back onto the machine that so tortured me I didn't bother naming him. I had gone in 2010 from my adorable Lil Red laptop to the nameless horror laptop to the peace of my Zenbook in 2012.

I booted up the nameless slug. I suffered through a morning of forced updates, check-disks, troubleshooting flaky internet connections, and locked screens. It felt oh-so-familiar. I thought about the manuscript files I needed to sift through and back up.

A thought snuck through my gloom (oh, traitorous brain) reminding me of all we—this piece of junk and I—had done together despite its many and obvious shortcomings.

I rebooted yet again after uninstalling a program that is a recurring bug on that infernal machine. It pops up every three months, and by pop up I mean *literally*, while I have a PowerPoint presentation projected onto a screen in front of a room full of paying customers, a "Please choose your language" box pops up. Whereupon inevitably one person in the class is an IT guy and he says, "Looks like you have a virus. I can fix that for you." And on break I let him think he does so, knowing full well I'll see my little friend again next quarter.

And that's when it hit me. That's when I just *knew*. I couldn't finish my WIP (work in progress) on the Zenbook. The fickle muse wanted me back on whatever the hell this machine's name was. I would have to put the 2.7-pound, sleek, fast, unbuggy Zenbook away for now and beat my head against the ten-pound, clunky, slow, infected monstrosity that . . . that . . . that . . . had yielded the best thing I had ever written.

Shit.

I was vanquished. I admitted defeat. My next novel emerged from her chrysalis on my battered silver monster.

"Let the words begin again," the muse said. And it was good.

I wish I could give you a cure for writer's block, but no such creature exists. The best advice I have is try to be flexible, persistent, and patient—and take comfort in your community, because even the best writers battle the muse.

12 • TRY NOT TO SUCK

Making sure your book is ready to publish

My friends—and after all these pages, I feel I can call you friends—there are things you must do before you publish. Hard things, time-consuming things. Things to protect your books from suckage. Things that, if you do them well, will make your book competitive with traditionally published books. Things that, if not done, will leave it languishing in obscurity.

Publishing is forever, so you'd better make it good.

A print book sold is permanent. An e-book? Sure, you can take an e-book off sale or substitute an updated version, but how many people take the time to replace their old one? Most people never reopen your book once they decide they are done, whether they reach the end or get fed up with errors or crappy writing. Only a few people recheck and reread, and they only do it for those rarest of authors, the ones whose books they love so much or find so useful that they reach for them over and over again. You won't be that author if your book sucks.

So it's time to talk about content and rewriting, critique groups and manuscript consults, the very things that help you write not just *a* book, but your best book, or at least the best you can achieve with that particular book.

[Note: Not every book written needs to be published. Reaching "The End" is not sufficient justification for killing trees and electrons. Just sayin'.]

Writing is rewriting.

Wrap your head around this. Rewriting means you write until "The End" and then, maybe after a breather of a month or three, restart at "Once upon a time." And do it again. And again. And again. Until your sculpture is more Rodin than Play-Doh.

An experienced agent once told me that *The Thorn Birds* went through ten rewrites. (Thanks, Elizabeth Pomada.) Have you ever picked up *The Thorn Birds?* It's hefty. Imagine rewriting that sucker ten times. But that's what it took, and, obviously, Colleen McCullough had the vision, patience, and work ethic to do it.

You need to, as well.

The rewrite process can be triggered at several points in the life cycle of a manuscript. First, I hope you rewrite it yourself as your ideas develop and you see the need arise. Feedback from critique partners can also trigger rewrites, as can advice received though a manuscript consult, an agent, or an editor.

Honest feedback is critical.

I simply can't imagine a book that wouldn't benefit from rigorous critiquing. Get your manuscript in the hands of people with the education and skills to provide you with meaningful feedback on story structure, plot, genre "rules," characters, consistency, plot-point plausibility, tension, pace, voice, dialogue, scene setting, and more. This isn't about your girlfriend correcting your grammar, folks. It's about someone kicking the living shit out of your manuscript's tires.

Round one: The inner circle

Friends, don't make people read your crappy first draft. OK, maybe on your first book, and then only people you really hate. Scratch that. Only people that love you enough to say, "Wow, awesome," and pretend they made it all the way through. Please, please, please go through it at least three times (writing your initial draft, rewriting the parts that don't work, and performing a substantive self-edit) before you subject it to the world. Then have a few trustworthy but gentle people give it a quick read to see if it's worthy of calling in chits. Make any suggested changes that you buy into. Then, and only then, in my opinion, should you ask writing groups or critique partners to wail on it.

Round two: Better writers than you

Ideally you can gain access to writers far better than you— published writers, talented writers, writers who can help you grow. Yes, you probably need to find better critique partners. I'm sorry.

Education and skills aren't the only criteria to judge critiquers by, however. It's also critical that your critiquers have the confidence and kindness to be open and honest with you. Meek is not a quality you're looking for, nor is protective. You need someone who can be honest without being brutal. Honest feedback may *feel* brutal, because we're sensitive about our book babies, aren't we? But the kindest thing you will ever receive is actionable feedback. Even if it stings to receive it.

And then set it aside for a cooling-off period, enough time to give you emotional distance. Think months, or at least weeks. Go back to it and re-edit.

Great critique partners are still—usually—unpaid, and while they are experienced, they may not be professionals at book consults. I don't know about you, but when I'm not paid, I tend to budget my time and effort accordingly. So with the help of your critiquers you'll kick your book up a notch, but for those of you shooting for the moon, you may want to add some BAM with a professional manuscript evaluation.

Round three: Professional readers

Manuscript evaluations go by many names: content edits, critiques, consults, and evaluations. Really, really substantive edits may rise to the level of a manuscript evaluation, but beware: any time you go through an edit, you are trying to achieve perfection. If, as a result of a deep substantive edit, you undertake further rewrites, you will have changed perfected sections, deleted them, or added new material. In other words, you run the risk of paying for editing twice.

My editor is a goddess and makes my books (and me) look good. Services offered in a manuscript evaluation vary, but they often address the same or similar elements as hers: plot, pacing, structure, character development, description, point of view, voice, and more. Evaluators charge by either the word, hour, or project, and most of them require half their fee up front. Many author-service providers offer evaluations, too. CreateSpace sells editorial evaluations for $199 and "comprehensive copy editing plus" for 2.2¢ per word. Freelancers run from 1–2¢ per word, or around $35–$65 per hour.

You can find great evaluators in a few ways. Check the acknowledgments in indie books you love. Most of them, like me, thank the editor and any others involved in polishing their book. You can try to hire mine—Meghan Pinson—but get in line (http://mytwocentsediting.com). You can also look for freelancers through referral sites (like http://elance.com) or professional organizations (http://the-efa.org/ and http://naiwe.com are two good ones). However you find yours, be sure to check references and review a sample finished product.

As you build your timeline, allow three months for a manuscript evaluation: one for the consult, one to incorporate the suggestions, and one for life getting in the way. However, you will need to book your evaluator months in advance. Most of the best ones have a wait list.

What makes a great critique?

Here's my personal perspective on critiquers, something I wrote a few years ago when I had finally found a great critiquer and understood the value of her input (thank you, Nikki Loftin, author of the fantabulous *Sinister Sweetness of Splendid Academy*):

As I mature (slowly) as a writer, the most important qualification I look for in a critiquer/reader is the courage to be honest. And when I say honest, I mean someone who will make me cry and send me into the fetal position.

I DON'T WANT TO HEAR WHAT'S RIGHT, I WANT TO HEAR WHAT SUCKS. WHAT BLOWS. WHAT BEGS TO BE DELETED. WHAT DESTROYS THE BOOK. BIG STUFF. IMPORTANT STUFF.

I don't care about commas. Periods. Capitalization. Spelling. Grammar. Spacing. Pagination. I taught writing in grad school. We all make typos. I can fix those with a painful day of spell/grammar/style check in Microsoft Word. Find/Replace is my friend. And then I'll have an editor to catch what I can't.

Instead, tell me what page you were on when you shut the book, when you went for a snack, when you fell asleep. I need information, like what irritates you about my protagonist. Really—how bad do you want to smack her upside her red-haired head? Hold that thought, write that page down. Tell me straight up, like it is. Hell, you can even call me if it's too bad for e-mail.

In order to be a good critiquer, you don't have to be an expert in writing, although that's a huge bonus. You need to be the one who is way past the use of "company manners." I'm looking for exclamation points after a capital N.O. I want OMG YOU CANNOT. I want PLEASE DON'T. I want WHAT WERE YOU THINKING.

Then, after you've pummeled me with those, you can tell me, "Way to go, kiddo. You took it like a champ, you rode that horse until it dropped. And you did it. Good job." Then, and only then.

Now, I love my mother and my husband. They're two of my favorite people. My husband, Eric, is a fantastic person to talk to about plot twists or to logic-check my scenarios for me. But he loves everything I write. He begs me not to delete things. I have to prove to him I saved the old draft before he will stop hovering when I thin a manuscript out. When my mother reads my manuscripts, her only comment is usually "Do you have to use the F word?"

Not very helpful. And yet every time I make improvements, they like it better. I'm not picking on them, I'm using them to make a point: too much praise will kill a story before it's born. I don't have time to write badly. Do you? Break up with your friends and get a critique group with teeth.

Guess what? I'm so scared about putting smelly poo out there that after I'm done with critiquers, I still pay for a manuscript consult with a book editor. Just like a traditionally published author gets from their house or press. And it's worth every penny.

13 • CHECK YOUR REFLECTION

Editing is everything.

Nothing turns readers off faster than badly edited books. They may hang in there with you for a few chapters if your story is weak, but they're gone in a flash if your copyediting is poor. Editing is *the* great differentiator, and this is the biggest knock I hear on indie books. Authors who don't heed these warnings—which are everywhere now—make the rest of us look bad. What makes them think substandard work deserves anyone's time or money? It's either ignorance or arrogance, but either way, it abuses the reader.

Copyediting and line editing are not about content. The last chapter focused on content. This chapter focuses on perfection, on ridding your manuscript of errors.

In this process, the editor does a number of things while preserving the meaning and voice of the original text. Copyediting includes:

—correcting mechanics (spelling, grammar, punctuation, syntax, and word usage)

—checking for or imposing a consistent style (Chicago, AP, APA, or MLA) for treatment of numbers and numerals, quotations, abbreviations and acronyms, italics and bold type, and more

—reading for overall clarity on behalf of your prospective audience

Get professional help.

You'll want someone top-notch for this stage. As with manuscript evaluation, indie authors often thank their editors in their acknowledgments. You can also find them through the same sites where you find manuscript evaluators (http://elance.com, http://the-efa.org, and http://naiwe.com). And my editor, Meghan, rocks at this, too (http://mytwocentsediting.com).

Whoever you use, be sure to ask for a sample edit. Not only do you want to see how your voice will be handled, but you also don't want to learn after the fact that your editor's revisions will take you a month of labor to decipher while you introduce new errors into the manuscript. Check references.

Many author-service companies offer editing. CreateSpace charges 1.2–1.6¢ per word. Freelancers will ask for half up front and charge by the word, job, or hour, usually between 1–2¢ per word. Higher rates are not uncommon, and the skill of the editor may warrant the cost. Build three months into your timeline for editing, but start that three months when you move to the front of your chosen editor's wait list. Because of this, I usually want my editor and cover artist working at the same time to cut down on my publishing timeline.

Maybe you are lucky and can barter for the services of a skilled editor, but however you pay for it, do not skimp on this stage. For pity's sake, do not do it yourself or allow anyone but a professional to do it for you. I would rather discourage you from publishing at all than let myself think that after reading *Loser*, authors pumped poorly edited books into an already crowded marketplace. Even though indie publishing has become easier, it's not without effort or cost.

Beta readers beget better books.

When your editor completes her work, you should not expect that your book is error-free. I've never seen one human capable of returning a completely error-free manuscript (http://americaneditor.wordpress.com/2013/07/31/the-business-of-editing-the-demand-for-perfection/). Instead, expect that it will have twenty errors or less. This is still not ideal for publication. All the published books I have ever seen, traditional and indie, have errors. But twenty is still too many. Your goal should be perfection, but in reality this is probably five or less.

So how do you eliminate those last fifteen? You're sick to death of your own words by this time and couldn't find errors in them if your life depended on it.

Enter the transcendent creatures I call beta readers. Beta readers take the final pass through your almost-finished product in return for the first read, your love and devotion, and possibly a mention in your acknowledgments. You want to find your most anal-retentive grammar-Nazi friends and readers for this job. My team consists of fans, friends, and family. My mom is on the team solely for ferreting out R-rated content. I usually veto her input, but she tries. My beta-friend Nan Loyd caught a staggeringly important error days before we printed 1,500 *Saving Grace* paperbacks. My beta-friend Rhonda Erb is so good with a red pen that she's now taking editing classes and pursuing a career as an editor. I know my manuscripts are ready to deem books after my betas have worked them over.

God bless them all.

PART THREE:
HOW TO PUT YOURSELF ON THE MARKET

14 • STRATEGIZE, YOU SEXY BEAST

Things to factor into your indie-publishing strategy

Strategy is sexy. A good one can give you the prescience that sends you home with a profit even when the pickings are slim.

The sexiest decisions you'll make when you indie publish?

1. Which formats to publish,

2. Where to publish, and

3. How to price.

Think of it as what you'll be wearing, where you'll be shaking it, and whether you want dinner and a movie first.

ISBNs: Baby, I got your number

In order to sell your book, you need your number on the bathroom wall. Your International Standards Book Number, that is. ISBNs are unique, country-specific numeric commercial book identifiers of ten or thirteen digits. Each edition, variation, and format of a book (except for reprintings) gets its own. For example, an e-book, a paperback, an audiobook, and a hardcover of a book will each have a different ISBN, with one exception; Amazon's Kindle and Barnes and Noble's Nook do not require e-book ISBNs. Because ISBNs are not free, this can be significant: if you plan to publish only e-books and only on those two sites, you don't need to spend a cent on ISBNs.

In the good old US of A, you can purchase ISBNs singly or in discounted volumes through Bowker (http://myidentifiers.com). You can also get ISBNs from some author-service providers if you list the service provider as your publisher. (We'll talk about that more later, I promise.) As you can see below, buying single ISBNs is quite pricey. Bowker's unit price falls dramatically with modest volume.

Buy 1 ISBN	$ 125
Buy 10 ISBNs	$ 250
Buy 100 ISBNs	$ 575
Buy 1000 ISBNs	$1000

DRM: It's who's in control

Cue the whips and handcuffs, baby, it's time to talk digital rights management. DRM is a controversial option that allows you to control access to digital formats of your copyrighted material—your e-books and audiobooks, for example. Some markets allow you to enable DRM on your e-book, but it's not entirely clear that this is a good idea.

Those who favor DRM believe it helps prevent theft, or piracy, of digital content. However, most of the major web-sales channels, including Kindle, Nook, Apple, and Kobo, strongly disfavor the use of DRM or even refuse to sell DRM-enabled books. Critics complain that DRM is overly restrictive and prohibits even legal use of digital content. Techies suggest that DRM doesn't do much to reduce piracy, since the type of users who would steal your content still can. Without going down that snake-infested rabbit hole, let me just tell you this: one of the fastest ways to get flamed on message boards is to enable DRM. I can't say I disagree with them. In fact, I'll go all out and say I believe DRM is a concept not yet ready for prime time.

Heck, people pass print books around and paw them until the pages wear out, and we're still buying those. How about instead of worrying whether people will steal your content, worry about whether they'll ever sit down and read your book all the way through at all? That's a much more realistic question. Then rejoice if someone reads it, lends it, and creates another fan for your next book. If you follow my reasoning, there's no need for DRM on indie books. So, at this time anyway, I highly recommend you do not enable DRM on your e-books.

In the next chapter, I'll bring the candles and champagne and we'll talk about e-book strategy.

And, no, I'm not just being a tease.

15 • ENGAGE IN DIGITAL STIMULATION

Strategy for e-books

E-books, my friends, tickle your readers' fancies. Whether or not to produce them is a no-brainer. As this book hits the shelves, e-book sales have gobbled up nearly 25% of the market for books—books of any and all kinds, according to Bowker. E-books present little to no per-unit cost or other fees to the author. They are increasingly easy to produce. The main strategic questions, then, are whether you will use an aggregator, which e-book formats you will offer, and where you will sell them.

E-books for indies

Amazon

In 2012, Amazon held around 60% of the e-book market with the sale of Kindle e-books. Heck, Amazon controls 27% of the book market overall. Not just e-commerce, but the *total* book market. Again, thank Bowker for this data. Talk about the one sales avenue you absolutely cannot ignore!

Why this massive market share for Amazon e-books? Well, for starters, they got there "first" with online book sales, e-readers, and e-books, and they make it easy by offering free Kindle apps for electronic devices. It's ubiquitous. I own a Kindle Fire. My eldest daughter has a Kindle Fire HD. My youngest son and middle daughter have iPads with Kindle apps on them. My youngest daughter uses a Kindle app on her iPhone.

Barnes and Noble

Amazon is not the only game in town; Barnes and Noble holds as much as 25% of the e-book market. Barnes and Noble updated its Nook e-reader with Google Play mid-2013, which enabled Kindle e-book apps for the first time. Smart move, Barnes and Noble. This makes the Nook more tablet-like.

My prediction? E-readers are out, tablets are in. E-readers that become tablets will stick around, and those that don't won't.

Apple

Apple has more than 10% of the market and is the real up-and-comer. Not only is Apple's iPad tablet an e-reader, but Apple sells e-books (and audio) directly through iTunes, which really appeals to the young adult market. Apple's strategy of allowing iPad owners to download the Kindle app is markedly different than Barnes and Noble's, and in my mind the wiser long-term approach.

The other guys

Next comes Kobo, which I think of—at least for now—as the indie-bookstore arm of e-book sales. I use Kobo and really like it. There are a slew of other options as well, including Google, Lulu.com, e-books.com, biblio.com, and omnilit.com, some of which are discussed in a good article on Examiner.com (http://www.examiner.com/article/where-to-upload-your-e-book).

We're going to focus on the Big Three (Amazon/Kindle, Barnes and Noble/Nook, and Apple/iTunes/iBooks) for the sake of simplicity. Trust me, if you can understand and navigate those three, you will be fine with the others, too. A quick Google search will yield more opinions if you want them. But first, let's explore aggregators.

Sales aggregators

Think of a sales aggregator as a simplifier: it will upload your e-book to many different online outlets in return for some of your revenue. There are a number of sales outlets that double as sales aggregators, but right now, I think BookBaby and Smashwords are the most significant players.

BookBaby

BookBaby charges a one-time per-book fee, and you keep 100% of the royalties paid by the booksellers. BookBaby will upload to a variety of sites, including Apple's iBooks/iTunes, Amazon Kindle, Barnes and Noble Nook, Sony, Kobo, and others. It also offers a number of author services, like cover design and editing, which you can read about on its website (http://www.BookBaby.com/).

Smashwords

I have a love-hate relationship with Smashwords, which I not-so-secretly call Aggregator Aggravator. I also know authors who swear by it, so maybe my frustrations are more about me. I'm good with that possibility.

Smashwords charges no up-front fee and offers no add-on author services. It uploads your e-book to all the usual sales outlets plus a few. It keeps 15% of the royalties paid by the online booksellers to whom it uploaded on your behalf. It also offers an affiliate-referral fee for sales that link from your website. Most of its retailers pay 60%.

If you allow Smashwords to imprint itself as the publisher of record on your e-book, you get a free ISBN. (Some e-book retailers, but not the Big Three, do require ISBNs.) Another nice feature of Smashwords is that it allows you to offer discount coupons for your e-books of up to 100%. That lets you leave your sales price intact and still give away books to selected individuals (which you can do on other sites using their Gift features, but you have to pay for the e-book in order to gift it). Since Amazon matches the lowest price on the web, protecting your pricing is important—you sure as heck don't want Amazon matching FREE.

While these perks are nice, they're offset by the difficulty of Smashwords formatting. Plan on following the instructions (https://www.smashwords.com/books/view/52) to the letter, and add a week to your timeline for wrestling with it the first time. Want to skip that aggravation? Pay someone $50 to do it for you. Smashwords provides referrals on its website (http://smashwords.com).

Should you aggregate?

My main aggravation with aggregation is that it may take weeks for changes to your pricing, availability, content, or description to show up on your booksellers' websites. This has hamstrung me many times.

If you aggregate, I think you should choose your provider based on your anticipated sales volume at your anticipated profit margin. Smashwords requires no cash outlay but keeps 15% of your sales price, and BookBaby charges a flat fee and keeps none of your sales price. And an up-and-coming aggregator called Draft2Digital is getting good buzz; it keeps 10% of your sales price, which beats Smashwords on pricing.

Wait, would that be easier to understand in a graphic?

Sales Aggregators Fees		
	Sales Price %	Flat Fee
Smashwords	15%	$0
BookBaby	0%	$99
Draft2Digital	10%	$0

To predict your profits, multiply your anticipated sales by your profit margin. Smashwords is cheaper if your profits will be lower than the one-time fee charged by BookBaby. BookBaby is the better deal if your profits will be higher than its fee. So, for instance, if you realistically expect to make $1 per e-book and to sell one hundred, then BookBaby at $99 (their fee as I write this) is the better choice for you.

Web-sales channels

Amazon's Kindle Direct Publishing (KDP)

KDP is the undisputed big kid on the block, and it's not just sales that make it king.

—The KDP website is easy to use (https://kdp.amazon.com/self-publishing/), even for neophytes.

—KDP doesn't require ISBNs for e-books. Whether you use an ISBN or not, all e-books are assigned an Amazon-specific identification number (an ASIN).

—You can upload a variety of file formats, like Word, PDF, or EPUB, but uploading a Kindle-compatible MOBI file yields the best results.

—E-books appear on Amazon within twelve to forty-eight hours of your initial upload.

—You can make changes with no fee, and they'll show up within twenty-four hours.

—Customer reviews on Amazon drive book sales on Amazon and elsewhere, and the system is very user friendly.

—KDP royalties are tops. In the US, Amazon pays 70% royalties (minus downloading and transmission fees) on e-books priced between $2.99 and $9.99 and 35% royalties on all others. Royalty rates vary among the 170+ other Kindle-friendly countries, but not by much. I'll give you a graphic of US royalty comparisons when I've finished explaining them for each of the Big Three. Oh, and if you're not from the US, I'm not being ethnocentric. I'm just sticking with what I know, and occasionally you'll have to translate my advice for your location. Lo siento.

—Buyers are allowed one lend of each purchased title.

—Sales reports are simple to generate and use.

KDP Select

Amazon's KDP Select program bears serious consideration. Basically, in return for giving Amazon a ninety-day renewable exclusive to sell your e-book, KDP Select gives you two great features.

Kindle Owners' Lending Library

The Kindle Owners' Lending Library (KOLL) is a free lending service available only to Amazon Prime members who own Kindle e-reader devices. Amazon sets aside a certain amount of money each month to pay authors for e-books lent through KOLL. Authors collect a percentage of this fund based on the number of their e-books lent compared to the total number of e-books from all authors lent for that month. For me, this amount has ranged from about $1.50 per lend to nearly $3 per lend. I find that lends do not rob me of sales, as buyers and borrowers constitute, for the most part, separate markets. In addition, the lends count toward Amazon sales rankings, which are a key driver of sales; the lends can actually end up driving more sales.

Free days

Normally, KDP does not allow book prices to be set to "free," but if the author participates in KDP Select, he can offer his title for free for up to five days of the ninety-day KDP Select period. Free days are a fantastic way to promote your e-book. Free downloads count as partial sales, so when you end your free days, you should experience a bump in your rankings, even among paid books.

Imagine 10,000 people downloading your book for free. Assume they read it and love it. What might they do for you? Recommend it to friends? Give it a 5-star review on Amazon? Both are awesome if they happen, and they often do. Still, many authors are afraid of giving away e-books.

This blows me away, since most of these authors don't have sales to speak of in the first place. People, hear me and hear me well:

—Habitual downloaders of free e-books work the system to a science. They weren't going to buy your book anyway. Most of the world doesn't bother to download free e-books—so most of the world is still in your potential paying-customer base, even if you do free days with KDP Select.

—A good performance on KDP Select free days may yield lasting rankings, sales, and Amazon promotion.

—Giving away a good book promotes reviews and word-of-mouth sales.

—Giving away an e-book does not rob you of sales when it's not selling anyway.

I'll quit shouting now.

Between the lends and the free days, I have seen fairly significant bumps in rankings during KDP Select periods. I also find that during these periods, sales take place on Amazon that might otherwise have occurred elsewhere. This further increases my Amazon rankings.

Barnes and Noble: PubIt!/Nook Press

Barnes and Noble's system is in flux as I sit here writing *Loser*. For the last few years, authors have used PubIt! to upload and manage their Barnes and Noble e-books. That system is still functional right now, but is being phased out in favor of Nook Press. First I'll address PubIt!, then the differences between it and Nook Press.

PubIt!

PubIt! (http://pubit.barnesandnoble.com) is very similar to KDP.

—Its website has an easy interface that allows uploads in several formats. EPUB works best and is the preferred format (as it is for Apple and Kobo).

—Barnes and Noble does not require an ISBN for e-books. It assigns a unique Barnes and Noble identification number, or BNID, to each title.

—Changes to manuscripts and covers are free.

—Sales reports are easy to generate and use.

—You can earn referral fees when buyers click through from your site.

—Buyers are allowed one lend per purchase of your book.

—Nook e-reader apps are available for free.

Some PubIt! features are different from KDP.

—Royalties are 65% for books priced $2.99 through $9.99 (lower than KDP) and 40% for all others (higher than KDP).

—PubIt! doesn't offer a select program.

—Barnes and Noble only sells online in the US and UK at the time of this book's publication, but has announced it will be adding eight more countries soon.

—Barnes and Noble's review system is poor—for PubIt! and Nook, and for e-books and all other products. It's cluttered with spam and legitimate reviewers report immense difficulty getting posts to stick. I don't guide my readers there anymore.

Nook Press

The new Nook Press (https://nookpress.com) has a snazzy new interface and online chat support, which is very nice. It allows you to write your manuscript online in posts similar to

WordPress or Blogger's, and you can invite editors and co-authors to collaborate with you.

Apple: iTunes, iBookstore, iBooks Author

Apple is unique. Like Nook Press, it uses an EPUB file. Unlike PubIt! and KDP, you have to upload your file using a specific type of machine. Yep, a Mac. And not just any old Mac. It must have a fairly recent operating system that will run Apple Producer. I love that Producer lets you schedule upcoming books; you can't do that with KDP or Nook Press. Sales are through iTunes and the iBookstore. Royalties are 60% across the board. You can access sales reports and perform other administrative functions through iTunes Connect (http://itunesconnect.apple.com) on any type of computer, and as with KDP, you can sell to markets all over the world.

I've found Apple far harder and more complicated to work with than any of the other web-sales channels, with the possible exception of Smashwords. They're neck and neck. The two of them are almost enough to drive me into BookBaby's aggregator arms—almost, but not quite. I'll endure almost any hardship for higher royalties.

One last complaint: in comparison to KDP, which e-mails you any time there's a tremor in the force, Apple is a really poor communicator. All messages about issues with your e-books come to you through iTunes Connect, so unless you go looking for trouble, you won't know it's found you. This doesn't sound like much of an issue unless you have print books in two places, audiobooks in one, and e-books in four, and are working with a bunch of brick-and-mortar stores, too. If everybody made you go hunt out problem notifications instead of e-mailing them directly to you, it would suck. Like it does with Apple.

Hey, Apple, I had to use my e-mail to set up my account—when are you going to start pushing notifications to me like it's the 21st century????

And I haven't even gotten into how much more onerous the up-front paperwork is with Apple. You have to *apply* to publish there.

Okay, it's beginning to sound like I don't love Apple, and that's not true. I do. It's a great sales channel, and they're innovators in so many ways.

Apple has a slick new feature that will appeal to lovers of technology: its iBooks Author allows you to create enhanced, interactive EPUB features. However, if you create your e-book with Author, it's exclusive to Apple unless you buy back your freedom for $15.

As e-readers disappear and tablets take over the world, iPad is leading the charge. This may be one of the reasons for the rapid growth of Apple in the e-book market. That's why, despite its great hassle factor, I direct-load all of my books with Apple. I want to make sure my books are poised to rise with Apple's iBooks star.

US Royalties, by comparison

Royalties	KDP	Nook	iBookstore
$2.99-$9.99	70%	65%	60%
Other	35%	40%	60%
Paid Lending?	Yes	No	No

Your own website

The upside of selling e-books on your own website? You get to keep all the money. The downside? The sales will not impact any web-sales-channels' rankings (which drive more sales), you'll have to provide your own customer support, and you'll have to drive traffic to your own site, which can be quite difficult. If you already get hits from millions of buyers for your products each month, though, this might be a good option for you.

Digital mastery

If you are going to sell your e-books on multiple channels, your most lucrative option is to upload to each one yourself. If you simply do not have the technical savvy or the time to manage them all, use an aggregator; compare your anticipated sales at your anticipated price to its royalties and/or fees.

Pro tip: Go with KDP Select.

I believe that right now, there is a benefit to the indie author to sell e-books through KDP Select. Here's why:

—Your Amazon sales, KOLL lends, and free Kindle downloads all impact your Amazon ranking.

—You'll earn KOLL revenues.

—Your books may be automatically promoted by Amazon if they sell well enough.

—Amazon's review system is robust and popular.

—Amazon.com has the world's largest market share of book buyers.

—A KDP Select ninety-day exclusive will simplify your life considerably.

Why are Amazon rankings so important?

Two reasons. First, some readers browse book rankings by genre to look for books to read. Amazon puts twenty books onto each page in these rankings. The closer you are to page one, the more likely a browsing customer is to run across your book. Second, Amazon will promote your book for you when it ascends from the nether regions of rankings, sales, reviews, and ratings—and automated promotion of your book can make it take off like a rocket.

Since I sell paperbacks in several bookstore chains and many indie bookstores, I try to keep my books available on the Big Three plus Kobo. That way, the customers who discover me in stores will easily find me online. Translation: I want shoppers in Barnes and Noble stores to find my Nook e-books on http://barnesandnoble.com. If I weren't on bookshelves, I might consolidate my sales on Amazon.

16 • GET HOT FOR HARD COPIES

Strategy for paperbacks

The advent of POD gave paperbacks a face-lift and a tummy tuck, and now they're feeling frisky. Producing paperbacks in small quantities is now affordable and accessible to authors.

Print is cheap and easy.

Since you're already going to invest in a perfect e-book manuscript with a great cover, the additional costs to print on demand with Amazon's CreateSpace are minimal. CreateSpace isn't your only choice for paperback printing, but it's great for indie authors who need fewer than 1,500 books. If you think you need more than that, look for an offset printer who offers volume discounts for short-run printing. And if you want to distribute to chain bookstores, consider Ingram's Lightning Source. (More on that later.)

Costs for e-book conversion through CreateSpace:

—$100–$200 to modify your e-book cover for paperback format

—\$50–\$100 to reformat the manuscript (or you can do it yourself for free)

Is it worth the expense? Paperbacks made up over 40% of the total book market in 2012. So you tell me.

Paperbacks get around.

For free

You'll use your books as gifts, giveaways, and review copies. You can't exactly leave an e-book in the seat pocket on an airplane for the next passenger to enjoy, but you can leave a mini billboard there. (And, really, how awesome is it to discover a literary gift from the gods when you're languishing in the electronicsless hell between doors closing and 10,000 feet?)

At events

I do a ton of direct sales at speaking engagements and public appearances; on average, about ten books per event. Obviously it varies by the size of my audience and the topic. I have 100% flexibility in the price I charge at these events, too. Anything above the print and shipping costs (which I'll talk about shortly) is gravy to me, so I usually offer discounts to make multi-book purchases attractive. I take cash, checks, and credit.

"Credit?" you shriek. "How do you handle credit cards?"

No need to get shrill. It's easy. Square Register turns my iPhone into a mini credit-card machine for 3% of each sale. *LOVE LOVE LOVE* Don't forget to work with your accountant to be sure you're following state laws.

When people carry your paperbacks around, other people can see them, ask about them, and borrow them. They are your business cards. Can an e-book do that for you? Not a chance.

Online

I direct customers to buy through web-sales channels because it maximizes my rankings—unless they want signed copies, which I am happy to sell myself. Ditto for a signed sticker to put in a paperback they've already purchased.

In bookstores

Brick-and-mortar bookstores command 18% of the book market. People often search for and find books by browsing in bookstores, even if they end up buying those titles as e-books instead.

Indie shops + indie authors = <3

Indie bookstores can be ripe for consignment arrangements, in which you leave your books in the store and they pay you periodically for the ones they've sold (or lost or destroyed). The majority of independent booksellers will accept your book on consignment if it's aesthetically pleasing, absent of glaring errors, and within the realm of what they sell. You can locate indie bookstores through Indie Bound (http://indiebound.com). Be sure to link to Indie Bound on your website to show your support if you want to work with them; they may also sell your books through its website. I'll talk about how that happens before the end of this chapter, I swear.

How to campaign for consignment

Prepare an inventory form (I've included one in the appendix) and pack a small box of your books, fliers, and bookmarks, then march cheerily into your favorite indie bookstore, preferably outside peak hours. Five to seven p.m. is good, as is the first hour after they open. Weekdays only. Offer them a free, signed copy of your book and your promotional materials for review in consideration of possible consignment. Chances are, they won't say yes on the spot, but you're ready if they do.

Consignment agreements

Most stores do a 60/40 split in favor of the author. This should cover your print and shipping costs, and it includes your profit. They can sell the book at whatever price they want to, but you should suggest one.

Note: I don't print retail prices on my book covers. Some experts recommend doing so, but I like being able to adjust prices with minimum confusion and hassle, and I let booksellers do the same. Also, making changes to the cover once a book is published sometimes incurs a fee. You'll make the call that seems best for you.

Some stores will charge a fee to carry your books by consignment, or even to evaluate and consider carrying them. You'll have to weigh the cost against the benefit of having your book in that store to know whether it's worth it to you. Keep in mind that publishers—major house and small press alike— pay for advantageous placement of their books in stores. It gets worse: those payments vary based on the type of placement, including new releases and even best sellers. No, this isn't a cruel joke. I once was given a guided tour of paid placement from a store manager at a major bookstore when I was there for a book signing of my own.

So it's no surprise that some booksellers charge indies a consignment fee. Be wary, though, when these fees get too high. Some bookstores have found they can make a better profit on desperate writers than they can from readers. If they charge you $100 to tuck three copies of your book away on some backroom shelf for three months, is that really worth it to you? It may be, but keep your eyes wide open and your index finger on the adding machine.

Keep the house happy

Once your book has been accepted for consignment, you need to drive sales to that store. Blog, e-mail, call, beg, and do whatever else you have to do to get people to buy your book at that store.

When we identify a store that we want to carry my books for the long haul, we send in a secret shopper from time to time to maintain steady sales. Remember, we get back 60% of the sales price, and 40% is a very small price to pay for the long-term value of having books in that store. Sometimes we donate the books purchased by our secret shoppers to the public library, and sometimes we place them where they can drive readers to more. We've dropped books on a library shelf at an indie coffee shop and in waiting rooms at doctors', dentists', and veterinarians' offices. We put a big fat sticker on the lobby copies that say "Available at Such and So Bookstore, 150 BuyLocal Drive!"

Keep good records and provide service to the store. Don't call them, interrupt what they are doing, or consume their time to ask how your book is doing. Go look for yourself. Wait until no customers are around so you're not a distraction, thank the booksellers for giving you shelf space, and ask them if there is anything you can do for them. Be sure you have books and promotional materials with you so you can fill those needs on the spot.

After you prove to the store owners that you generate sustainable sales, ask them to consider stocking your book through direct purchase. In order for them to agree, they'll need one additional incentive—and this is where careful pricing comes into play. Make sure the wholesale price is less than your consignment price. Otherwise, why would they accept the risk and hassle of ordering directly from you?

Paperback publishers: the main contenders

Amazon's CreateSpace

Excellent for online sales

CreateSpace lets you offer your print books at very competitive prices through standard Amazon channels that include the US, Europe, and Canada. You can pay an extra $25 for expanded distribution to other booksellers and libraries. Note that CreateSpace doesn't *market* to this expanded network for you; I've found expanded distribution nearly worthless, unless all you want is for Indie Bound to list your books on its website—and even Indie Bound prefers Lightning Source, as discussed below.

Bad for bookstores and libraries

Brick-and-mortar bookstores don't play nice with Amazon, and even if Ingram lists your books, most bookstores do not stock books that are POD unless they are fully returnable; CreateSpace does not provide for book returns. Libraries operate on very limited budgets, are generally quite selective when acquiring new books, and are very price sensitive. Think best sellers and volume discounts, not untested indie books.

No-nonsense fees

CreateSpace charges no fees other than the per-book printing costs. Uploading your print-ready interior and cover files is free—even uploading replacement files, no matter how many times you tweak the cover or interior. (Generally speaking, print-ready means that your interior is formatted for a book and saved as a PDF, and that your cover is created to CreateSpace specifications and saved as a PDF.) CreateSpace does not give volume discounts, but it offers a variety of shipping options.

Higher royalties

Generally speaking, your royalty for the same-priced book sold online through CreateSpace is twice that of a sale in a bookstore through Lightning Source, because bookstores expect you to sell to them at very low prices.

When your book sells on CreateSpace, CreateSpace subtracts its printing cost. When your book sells on Amazon, CreateSpace subtracts both its printing cost and Amazon's cut. You get the rest.

Pricing

CreateSpace lets you adjust the price of the book as you see fit on a handy screen that calculates your splits. You can purchase your own copies for the cost of printing—approximately 1.5¢ per page. (My books cost me $3–5 apiece plus shipping.)

Quality

It pains me to say it, but I have found the quality of CreateSpace's paperbacks inconsistent. We have had to return boxes of books due to blank pages, blurred print, odd coloration on the cover, missing pages, and poor binding. This is disconcerting, since we never see the books that are shipped to customers who ordered on Amazon. We have ordered thousands of books from CreateSpace and will continue to do so, but we check every book when they arrive, and we know that even the best of them will never look as good as the ones from Ingram.

Services

CreateSpace also serves up a suite of author services, including editing, covers, and marketing. Some of them are priced fairly competitively, others less so. You'll be able to decide for yourself if any of them make economic sense for you after reading some of the pricing guidelines in this book.

Ingram's Lightning Source

Best for bookstores

If you really want to get traction with booksellers, you should consider using Lightning Source for paperbacks sold everywhere but Amazon. Why? Because Lightning Source is owned by Ingram, the 800-pound gorilla of print-book distribution. All (or most) roads to brick-and-mortar stores lead through Ingram.

Returns give you options

Lightning Source lets you assume the risk of refunding books returned by booksellers if you want to. While this means you have to be smart and not spend all your royalty money on a wild trip to Vegas with your girlfriends, it provides much more incentive for stores to order your books. Returned books can either be destroyed or sent to you.

Pay to pulp

Pulping books is a regular practice in the publishing industry. In fact, some of those *New York Times* best sellers reach their exalted status by publisher-driven strong-armed mega orders from bookstores. Any books that don't sell are subject to return, or pulping, meaning the pages are returned to a pulp state and recycled into more paper and books. But that's long after the book is listed as a best seller, of course.

If you specify that your returns will be destroyed, then Lightning Source charges you what the bookseller paid for your book. When the bookstore ordered, you were paid only the royalty on the book. So for returns, you end up paying back far more than you made.

Pay to reclaim

If you specify that your returns will be shipped to you, Lightning Source charges you what the bookseller paid, plus shipping. You're out a little more, but you have the opportunity to do something with the books you've had to pay for anyway. If that's important to you, choose return/deliver.

No returns = no Barnes and Noble orders

You can also choose not to allow returns. You just won't get many bookstore orders. And—listen up, this is important—Barnes and Noble purchases from Ingram. So if you want to get into any of its 700 or so stores, Lightning Source is calling your name. And even then, it's still hard to break into the chains. See chapter 35 for more on this topic.

Fussy fees

Lightning Source offers volume discounts for printing and shipping, so if you order in large quantities, you'll achieve significant savings. In fact, you can even do short-run printing with them on orders of 2,000 or more books for mega savings.

Also, the $75 setup fee is waived if you purchase one hundred copies of your book.

One significant disadvantage to Lightning Source is that it charges a fee every time you want to replace your interior or exterior files. Change your cover? $40. Change the guts of your book? $40? Do both? $80. Do them both again a year later? $80. And Lightning Source is not nearly as easy to use as CreateSpace, so it's common to mess something up and find yourself needing to replace a file at $40 a pop.

Lower royalties

Lightning Source recommends that you give a 50–55% discount to booksellers, which means lower royalties for you. But booksellers' profits come out of the difference between your discount and the cut the distributor keeps, and I've found that some bookstores won't even buy my books unless I offer them a discount of 55% or more.

Bonus pain

Last but not least, you have to set up as a small press or work with an established press to work with Lightning Source. Doing this is not incredibly difficult, but it is a hassle. Lightning Source ain't for neophytes.

My favorite paperback strategy: Double down.

If you're serious about print books, really serious, I recommend working simultaneously with Lightning Source (allowing returns) and CreateSpace (without expanded distribution). That will earn you the best possible royalties from print sales in bookstores and on Amazon. Repurposing your CreateSpace materials for Lightning Source is fairly painless. You'll have to make minor modifications to the cover and pay $75 for a book setup fee plus $12/year to be in Lightning Source's ordering system, but the per-book print costs are about the same as for CreateSpace.

The popular paperback track: Keep it simple.

Let's get real. Most indie authors need only Amazon's CreateSpace. This is the route that is simplest and requires the least investment, because, c'mon, life is too short for most of us to jack around with complications. What's more, if you don't care about making a profit, you can put your book wherever you want in whatever format you want, then focus on living the dream and having a blast.

The fastest way to lose money is to over-order paperback inventory, so order only the books you know you will need. The cheapest shipping takes about two weeks. Have enough books on hand to sell at speeches and events, for review copies, and for giveaways. Multi-title authors should give away *lots* of their first few books. Single-title authors should give away fewer. I'll discuss giveaway strategy more later.

If you want to go for the brass ring, revenue-wise, expect to encounter a complicated and changing array of options for paperback sales.

17 • WHISPER IN MY EAR

Audiobook strategy

Video killed the radio star, or so sang the Buggles in 1979. But we still listen to radio, and we still read books, and we listen to audiobooks, too, more and more every year.

No discussion of strategy is complete without a word on audiobooks, which have become so simple and cheap to produce that they join the ranks of e-books as no-brainers, in my opinion.

Audible's Audio Creation Exchange is your new BFF.

Author, let me introduce you to Audible's Audio Creation Exchange (ACX, at http://acx.com). **ACX**, meet the indie author. On ACX, an author can search for narrators, many of whom will work for 50% of the audiobook's future royalties. I've been very pleased with ACX's wide variety of talented narrators, and I am thrilled with the final products of my six completed audiobooks. My only cost was for my digital artist to adapt my e-book covers to the audiobook parameters.

You can get the highest royalties by selling exclusively through Audible and its partners. Those royalties vary so widely that you'd do best to look them up yourself on ACX (http://acx.com). In addition, if a new customer signs up for Audible and chooses one of your books in her first three purchases, Audible pays a $25 bonus. That's music to my ears, no matter the format.

18 • DO IT FOR MONEY

How to price your products

It's time to talk about dirty, sexy money. Not all of you are publishing to turn a profit, but many of you are. One of the hardest choices you will face is how to price your books and e-books. Why? Because it is so hard to see whether your pricing strategy is helping or hurting you amongst the many other variables that might be impacting sales. I've read tons of advice from luminaries in the field, and most of it is conflicting: Price your e-books at 99¢. Price your e-books at their level of quality. Price your e-books to undercut major houses but high enough to keep 70% margins.

E-book pricing

Let's start with e-books. Some indie authors—like Amanda Hocking—have been incredibly successful at profiting from volume by charging 99¢ for e-books. Amazon pays a 35% royalty for books falling outside the $2.99–$9.99 range and a 70% royalty for books falling within it. Low prices can be very appealing. But some buyers will associate low cost with low quality, and many authors want to make more than 30¢ per sale, so there's a good argument for higher prices. Theoretically, pricing e-books between $2.99–$9.99 (in Amazon's highest royalty range), sends a message of quality.

Theoretically, anyway.

Does your book have the potential for high-volume sales? Is it *The Secret History of Rhode Island Basket Weavers?* Maybe not. But a romantic YA novel about an angsty teenage girl? Possibly. Ask someone knowledgeable about the book industry, like a bookseller or an agent at a writers conference, because you're not exactly an objective bystander concerning your own work. If your book is a good candidate for high-volume sales, offer it for 99¢.

If you're going for higher royalties because you're expecting lower volume, you have more to consider. First, you should come in lower than similar, traditionally published books because you can beat them on price without all the middlemen and -women. And, like it or not, "brand" has value. Penguin is a brand. You are not (yet). I may not be able to taste the difference between generic ketchup and Heinz, but Heinz is more valuable in the minds of consumers, so it carries the higher price.

Second, shorter books should hover at the lower end of the range. Full-length indie fiction generally runs in the $2.99–$5.99 range, but you will see it as high as $7.99 and up if it's brand new and by someone with a great name and reputation. One way to incentivize readers to buy your serial fiction is to price the first book at 99¢ and the newer titles at a higher price, with the highest reserved for the current release. As the book ages, the price may fall, especially for series fiction; in my experience, nonfiction prices hold up better over time than fiction prices.

Another way to incentivize buyers is to bundle your complementary books into one e-book and offer it at a discount. Web-sales channels will sometimes offer your complementary books at lower prices if they're purchased together; when this happens, you get your full royalty. Sweet. Unfortunately, when you bundle them and offer them for a discount yourself, the web-sales channel pays the royalty for the bundled price. But even if you don't bundle them, sometimes readers who dig you will buy your whole library of complementary titles at once. Truly, fortune favors the multi-title author when it comes to impulse buys.

Paperback pricing

It's difficult to compete on price with traditionally published paperbacks. For one thing, you probably won't ask less than cost, which is generally printing plus shipping. For another thing, you don't have the tremendous economies of scale the traditional houses do. You won't be able to match their prices for mass market paperbacks, even without the middlemen. But you should come as close as you can.

If your books are carried in stores, you can't let your online prices undercut brick-and-mortars by so much that your store sales tank. Amazon will match the lowest online price, which is always cheaper than stores (unless you're in the $1 bin). Whether Amazon's lower price will divert customers from bookstores is a question of how much cheaper Amazon is, really, because some people prefer to shop brick-and-mortar even at a slightly higher price. A few even insist upon it.

Your e-books will be cheaper than your paperbacks, and this is less of a threat to stores. Certainly e-books themselves are a threat—I double dog dare you to start talking about the Kindle edition of your book in Barnes and Noble or some hip indie shop—but your e-book pricing does not go head-to-head with your in-store paperback pricing. To the best of your ability, try to match the cost of other indie print books in your genre. Then discount your fiction about six to nine months after its debut. Leave your nonfiction pricing alone unless it's not working. Discount as it ages if you feel it's necessary to stimulate sales.

Case study: Yours truly

Time to show you my bloomers.

E-books

My 40,000-word nonfiction e-books retailed for $3.99 in their first year, after which I dropped them to $2.99. My 80,000-word novel debuted at $4.99; at seven months, I dropped it to $3.99. When I launched my next fiction release—a 90,000-word series mystery—at $3.99, I dropped the first book in the series to 99¢. I felt each book performed above expectations.

Paperbacks

My 40,000-word nonfiction paperbacks retailed for $12.95 in their first year, after which I dropped them to $10.95. My 80,000-word novel debuted at $18.95; at seven months, I dropped it to $12.95. However, because I wanted to be more competitive, I launched my next fiction release—a 90,000-word series mystery—at $16.95.

As discussed earlier, while Lightning Source urges that the standard discount is 50–55%, we've found that some bookstores don't get a "standard" discount from Ingram if we go lower than 55%, and thus would not order from us. We set discounts at 55% and allowed returns with Lightning Source.

Remember, Amazon will always match the lowest price on the web, so be careful. This price-matching demands some complex strategy when you're publishing POD through both CreateSpace and Lightning Source. As each company adjusts its policies, best practices for authors change. Amazon, especially, is constantly tweaking its inventory and pricing policies, so what is true today will not likely stay that way very long. For a fantastic article on strategy as of the time I wrote *Loser*, visit Aaron Shepard's Publishing Page (http://www.newselfpublishing.com/PlanB.html).

PART FOUR:
HOW TO FAKE IT TILL YOU MAKE IT.

19 • WORK YOUR IMAGE

Covers are your books' business cards.

Devotees of marketing guru Seth Godin will love this nugget: Your cover is your brand, and if you want to make it easy for your tribe to help you promote it, it needs to be a darn good one. Some of us are lucky and married to a digital artist who can do covers for free. (Not me.) Others can barter services in exchange for a great cover. The rest of us either do them ourselves or pay for them.

Hire a pro.

If you're paying, I can't imagine you'll get a cover you love for less than $250. Expect the range to be $250–$1,500. Digital artist extraordinaire Heidi Dorey charges me something in the middle of that for a package that includes e-book, CreateSpace, Lightning Source, and audiobook covers. I know people who spend double what I do. If you don't have a Heidi in your life, you'll have to hunt your artist down. Some good places to start?

—Post a job at http://elance.com

—Join the discussion on Goodreads about cover artists (http://goodreads.com/topic/show/837698-book-cover-artists-illustrators)

—Jump on the Kindle Boards and look for referrals

—Go to Savvy Self-Publishing for tips and resources (http://www.savvyselfpublishing.com/editing-art-formatting/how-to-get-cover-art-for-your-book-or-e-book)

Design is intentional.

No matter the method you choose, you need to understand what makes a cover original, clear, evocative, and memorable—or not—and why. You need to keep in mind that your other book-related imagery, like bookmarks, posters, and web banners, will build off your cover. Also, you have to embrace the truth that great covers must work equally well in full size and as an approximately 100x150-pixel thumbnail on a laptop screen in a list of books on Amazon.

Your cover should be original.

That being said, libraries of good-quality stock images are great resources. They offer a wide variety of existing work, you pay a small fee to use the image, and the artist profits from her work. You'll receive an image that can be edited in programs like Adobe Photoshop (expensive) or Gimp (free at http://gimp.com). If you decide to use stock images, consider altering them in some way to make your cover unique.

Your cover should be clear.

The title of the book and your name are the most important elements of your cover. If an image works with them to attract readers, great. If the imagery is so complex that it overwhelms your name, title, and message, or if it confuses people, then dump some of the detail and go with the power of simplicity.

Your cover should be evocative—

—and the feeling you want to evoke is "Damn, I need to buy

that book right this second." You are using color, fonts, and images to create a representation of your book—a symbol of it—that will appeal to readers who are about to discover that they can't live without what you wrote.

Your cover should be memorable.

Most readers don't buy a book the first time they see it unless they know the author or it was recommended by someone they trust. You want a cover that gets branded on their brains so that by the second or third time they see it, they experience a positive association with it. And then buy it.

To gather ideas, walk through a bookstore and browse covers in your genre. Which ones grab you? Why? Which ones don't? Why? Which ones repel you? Do they look cheap? Bland? Rushed? Then pull up the best sellers in your genre on Amazon. Do the same thing at thumbnail size—and don't cheat and pull up the book page. Which thumbnail-sized covers pull you in, and why, and which don't? Discover for yourself what the key cover elements are and why they work.

Time it right.

I don't like to start a cover until my book goes to copyediting. Why? Because until I process all the feedback from a manuscript consult and my critiquers, I still face the very real possibility of making substantial changes. Of a potential rewrite. Of throwing the stinker in the dipsy dumpster. That great idea you had for the cover might not work now that Earth doesn't explode at the end.

It's a good idea to allow for several months between the time you discuss concepts with your graphic artist and the time you upload your cover for printing and e-book distribution. Does that seem like a long time? For starters, you probably won't cut to the front of the line with the graphic artist, and real life can get in the way for you both. The less experience each of you has, the longer it will take. Here are some things you can do to speed up the timeline:

—Book your artist in advance

—Collect samples of covers or images that you like (http://bookcoverarchive.com is a good source)

—Collect samples you don't like

—Convey with simplicity and clarity what you want your artist to create

If the earth doesn't move for you when you see the cover, keep working on it. You're more likely to love it than anyone else, and if you don't, that's a problem.

Good covers say "Buy now." Bad covers say "Next, please." What will yours say?

20 • GIVE GOOD COPY

Cover and web copy sell books (or not).

As you gently maneuver your potential buyer closer and closer to clicking Add To Cart, your next speed bump is copy. Think of copy as the description of your book that appears underneath it on Amazon. It's often the same as, or quite similar to, the words on the back of the book, which are called back-cover copy.

Copy is *not* a synopsis of your book. It's more like a pitch— you know, like the ones we practice giving at writers conferences, where you sell an agent on the idea of your book in a couple of breathless sentences? But it's more than that. It's giving that pitch in the same tone you wrote your book in, and leaving the potential reader intrigued by the best bits and dying to know more.

For all of you who have slaved over query letters and thought you would be done with them forever if you went the indie route, au contraire. Because remember that sparkly hook and paragraph you wrote in hopes of snagging an agent? Yeah, the stuff you sweated over and cried over and swore was harder to write than your whole damn book? It's a lot like good copy.

Let me give you an example. Here's the copy from Amazon for *The Sinister Sweetness of Splendid Academy* by Nikki Loftin:

Lorelei is bowled over by Splendid Academy—Principal Trapp encourages the students to run in the hallways, the classrooms are stocked with candy dishes, and the cafeteria serves lavish meals featuring all Lorelei's favorite foods. But the more time she spends at school, the more suspicious she becomes. Why are her classmates growing so chubby? And why do the teachers seem so sinister? It's up to Lorelei and her new friend Andrew to figure out what secret this supposedly splendid school is hiding. What they discover chills their bones—and might even pick them clean!

Isn't that great? The idea is to entice the reader and leave him hanging.

Copy can be fairly short. Here's mine from *Leaving Annalise*:

One unexpected and hotly fought-over little boy, two dead bodies, and a series of home vandalisms throw Texas attorney turned island chanteuse Katie Connell into a tizzy. Juggling all of this, Bloody Mary cravings, baggage, and the bad guys, too, she waffles between the jumbie house that brought her back from the brink and the man she believes is the love of her life.

And from Stephen King's *The Stand*:

A patient escapes from a biological-testing facility, unknowingly carrying a deadly weapon: a mutated strain of super-flu that will wipe out 99 percent of the world's population within a few weeks. Those who remain are scared, bewildered, and in need of a leader. Two emerge—Mother Abagail, the benevolent 108-year-old woman who urges them to build a peaceful community in Boulder, Colorado; and Randall Flagg, the nefarious "Dark Man," who delights in chaos and violence. As the dark man and the peaceful woman gather power, the survivors will have to choose between them—and ultimately decide the fate of all humanity.

Since *The Stand* is more than three times as long as my *Leaving Annalise*, I think you'd still have to call this pitch short.

Good copy captures the essence of your conflict and gives the reader a taste of your style, characters, and setting. Writing it takes practice—and a lot of migraine meds. But you can't sell books without it, so accept your fate and buckle down.

Finish your copy before your graphic artist starts working, because she will need it for the back cover. Even if you're not doing print, you'll still need it before you upload an e-book anywhere. At the very latest, draft it while the interior of your book is being formatted. I budget two weeks to a month for writing copy, because I need time for several iterations with my critiquers and editor.

Oh, and a word of warning for the corner cutters: treat copy like the book itself. Don't even think about publishing it without critique and editing. It's the first example of your writing that readers will encounter, and if it's sloppy, they're going to move on down the road.

21 • PRETEND YOU'RE A ROCKET SCIENTIST

How to format e-books

The thought of formatting e-books sends most authors into the shakes. Deservedly so, because in the past, it was quite difficult. But not anymore. Not at all. You don't even have to do it yourself if you don't want to.

For starters, if you want to punt on the whole process, you can go with an aggregator like BookBaby or Draft2Digital (but not Smashwords, whose requirements are hellish in and of themselves). Or, even easier, you can upload a print book (as a Microsoft Word or PDF file) into CreateSpace and for $69 let them convert it to an e-book and put it on Kindle for you. But beware, your e-book will be exclusive to Amazon if you do so.

You can also hire someone to format your e-book for you. Get on the schedule early; many of them have a backlist. Budget two weeks for the formatter to get it back to you, and expect to spend between $50 and $150. Fiction is easier and thus less expensive. Some nonfiction is so complex due to images, tables, lists, bullets, footnotes, or, gasp, text boxes, that formatters will ask more than $150. If you want to find a formatter, try the Kindle Boards (https://kdp.amazon.com/self-publishing/help?topicId=A3RRQXI478DDG7) and Goodreads discussion groups (http://www.goodreads.com/topic/show/1184235-formatting-services). Or just Google "e-book formatting services" and wade through the masses.

If you're computer savvy, give it a try yourself. Don't be frightened. You won't need to go crazy with a bunch of HTML. You can make it as hard or as easy as you would like.

I format by the law of diminishing returns, meaning that I don't invest any more effort for features than I think their value to the reader warrants. Anything I invest past the point of high value to my readers has a diminishing return.

Formatting for beginners

For e-books, some of the formatting elements you are used to in print and in Word documents won't be relevant. Page breaks? There are none. Font size? Your reader can change it. Same thing with the colors of your page and text, so don't even worry about them.

What elements are important to readers of e-books? Leaving aside a good cover, great editing, and a fantastic book, of course, an e-book reader expects the same reading experience as a print reader. She'd also like front matter like acknowledgments and dedications moved to the back of the book. She wants active hyperlinks, and images that are either hyperlinked or can be enlarged. She would like the table of contents hyperlinked to corresponding sections. Most other bells and whistles mean nothing to the masses; at least, not yet.

Some ways of doing all this are harder than others.

Thus, while former Apple man Guy Kawasaki raves about Adobe Illustrator for the creation of e-books and sings the praises of the new enhanced e-book features available through

Apple's iBooks Author, I'm not sold that the extra trouble is worth it, especially for fiction. If you are, then I highly recommend you check out his book *Author, Publisher, Entrepreneur*, where he covers it in a little more detail. Not enough to teach you how to use Adobe Illustrator or iBooks Author, though—you'd need to get your hands on something more specific for that. Even Mr. Kawasaki admits that it was his co-author, tech wizard Shawn Welch, who taught him what he knows about Illustrator.

If Adobe Illustrator is not for you and you still want to go all crazy with HTML, by all means, do it. You could end up with a fantastic e-book. There's a great how-to available on David Gaughran's website and in his e-book, *Let's Get Digital* (http://davidgaughran.wordpress.com/lets-get-digital).

I like things simple.

I'm looking for a simpler experience, where for a low investment of dollars and time I can create a high-quality, nice-looking e-book. There are a variety of ways to achieve this, and your choice circles back to strategy, that sexy beast. What's your strategy for selling your e-books? Will you sell them through Amazon? Barnes and Noble? Apple? Kobo? Your website? Your strategy determines which file formats you'll create.

The simplest method: pay someone.

The simplest method is to publish your e-book exclusively through KDP when you publish the paperback through CreateSpace. All you have to do is pay a fee, and CreateSpace will convert the file to an e-book and load it onto KDP for Amazon sales.

DIY, simple and free

A method I like better than paying CreateSpace: you can upload your Word file straight to KDP *for free*. You don't need any special software or equipment, and KDP's Word converter does a decent job. However, if you want a hyperlinked table of contents, then you'll need to create them in Word using bookmarks and hyperlinks—*not* Word's automated Table of Contents, which not all converters like. (Word's Help feature provides instructions on how to do this.) I also strip out headers, footers, page breaks, and section breaks before I let KDP do a Word conversion.

Once you upload your Word file to KDP, you can check your file online before you "go live" to see how it looks and what functionality you have (or don't have). Then you fill out all the blanks in KDP's online submittal form, upload your cover, and hit Publish. A few days later, your book pops up for sale on Amazon, and you can start earning full royalties at 70% or 35%, depending on your price. And you didn't have to create a single e-book yourself, although ideally you followed my lead on some special formatting in Word, like the hyperlinked Table of Contents.

Barnes and Noble's PubIt!/Nook Press offers a similar Word converter, as do Apple and Kobo. None of the web-sales channels charge fees for their converters.

DIY for control freaks

If you want greater control of how your e-book looks and functions, you can format it yourself and upload the files to the various sites. I like me some control, but I don't let things get too complicated. I use a WordPress-based service called PressBooks (http://pressbooks.com).

I like PressBooks because I blog using WordPress, and, thus, for me, PressBooks is a walk in the park skipping along a wooded path singing tra-la-la and picking daisies. You simply create chapters like you create blog posts—by clicking Add New and typing or copying in your chapter text, then hitting Save—and PressBooks automatically formats them for you. You add in front and back matter in the same way. You enter your book's information and cover, then you choose between some simple e-book choices, like indented paragraphs (fiction and narrative nonfiction, mainly) versus skipped lines between paragraphs (usually for nonfiction, although I break the rules on this from time to time because I prefer this format, even for fiction), and click Export.

PressBooks creates MOBI, EPUB, and PDF files that you can download and use wherever you want. If you want, you can use those files to become a BookBaby aggregation customer, subject to standard BookBaby fees, and then sell them through a PressBooks-generated site that operates like your personal website. Its sites look really nice, but I don't use one because I don't need to give fees to aggregators and I built my own website, which I'll address later.

Voilà. An hour with PressBooks (for fiction; nonfiction takes much longer), and I have the files I need for Amazon (MOBI), Barnes and Noble (EPUB), Apple (EPUB), and Kobo (EPUB), with a look and functionality that meets my standards. Yes, I could have created e-books with an even more customized look and additional features using HTML, Illustrator, or iBooks Author, but I don't think my readers are clamoring for this in the types of books I write. The only downside to me, and it's a small one, is that there is a notation in my e-book that it was created with PressBooks. Well, I got the service for free, so why not? If it bothers you, you can strip the watermark from MOBI and EPUB files for $10, and in those plus the PDF for $100 .

DIY for the indie who wants everything

If for some reason you want additional file formats, like for uploading to web-sales channels like OmniLit (http://omnilit.com) that sell e-books in every imaginable obscure format, that's easy, too. Download the free Calibre software (http://calibre-e-book.com). Open your e-book in Calibre, then convert it to any format you wish. I like to use Calibre to preview all my e-book formats. Note that you cannot start from a Word document in Calibre, but you can start from just about any e-book format.

And there's a new word-processing program designed specifically for authors that everyone and their long-legged brothers are talking about: Scrivener (https://www.literatureandlatte.com/) lets you create everything from manuscripts to e-books to blog posts, for $40. I haven't used it yet, but I plan to try it soon; it's getting rave reviews (http://michaelhyatt.com/switched-to-scrivener.html).

So, e-book formatting is as easy or as hard as you want to make it. Allow two weeks in your timeline. Expect to spend $50–150 if you hire it out.

Capisce?

22 • GET YOUR NAME IN LIGHTS

Formatting paperback books

Nothing can replace holding your print book in your hands for the first time. Forget babies, puppies, and your beloved's . . . hand. Print book, yours: awesome.

As you already know, I am a huge advocate of print books for indie authors. And not just because they will legitimize you with your friends and family when they see your work in print (which they will), but because they have *legs*. I've already preached on that topic, though, so let's talk about how to format your manuscript for print production.

How to format print books

First, use Word, and preferably create .doc manuscripts instead of .docx, as .docx doesn't yet work for all the people and software you may use in the formatting stage. Play to the lowest common Word version as your denominator.

Once upon a time, I formatted five nonfiction manuscripts for e-book and print at one time. As a result of living through that hell, I vowed that when typing a manuscript,

1. I would never use the Tab key again (those of you who have self-published are smiling right now),

2. I would only use Word (.doc, not .docx), and

3. I would always use Styles. If you don't know what I mean, you need a quickie class on Word, and I recommend you go take one online.

Some things you just need to trust me on, OK?

The easy way: pay someone.

With interior formatting for print, as with e-books, you can make it as easy or as hard as you want. Want to go the easy route? Hire someone! If you hire out, expect to pay $50 for standard fiction and up to $300 for complex nonfiction layouts. Goodreads discussions on formatting are a good place to find referrals (http://www.goodreads.com/topic/show/1184235-formatting-services), and I really like a formatter at a website called Go Published (http://www.gopublished.com/). Your e-book formatter can often do your print formatting, too.

Author-service companies like CreateSpace offer print formatting, but they charge from $249–$400, which I think is highway robbery. Unfortunately, many neophytes go to CreateSpace before reading a book like this one, and they see that CreateSpace can make it easy for them, and they think, "$250? Why not? I can make that back in book sales." Robbery, I say.

If you decide to pay someone to format your book for print, add two weeks into your timeline, unless your service provider has to wait-list you. It's always wise to book in advance.

DIY with templates

There are two ways to format your e-book with templates: with templates provided by web-sales channels and without them. Let me show you what I mean.

CreateSpace has Word templates for whatever size book you want to create, and you can import the resulting files into Lightning Source, too. The most common size is 6x9, and I use it for my novels. I use 5.25x8 for my nonfiction books, which are shorter. These templates are handy if you are very proficient in Word; if not, they are easy to mess up. I'm pretty Word savvy, and on my first try at interior formatting I got turned sideways and couldn't recover. I have since successfully used CreateSpace's templates, but I had better luck with Book Design Wizard.

If you want to remain independent of the web-sales channels, try using Book Design Wizard 2.0 (http://www.self-pub.net/wizard.html) or something similar. Book Design Wizard is a $39.50 piece of software that is nothing more than a really snazzy Word template, but far more Pamela-proof than the CreateSpace version. Their customer service is good, too— as is CreateSpace's, with which I've had a wonderful experience.

Choose the method you find easiest to use.

DIY from scratch

You could format your paperback yourself in Word from scratch, but unless you know all the rules of formatting interiors, it's guaranteed to mark you an amateur. Some of the most common beginner missteps involve headers, widows and orphans, fonts, line spacing, and indents. In fact, I think I violated some of the rules about these elements on my first try.

If you want more information on interior formatting rules, CreateSpace has a lot of support documents with tips, so many that I encourage you to click on its Free Publishing Resources drop-down and check out the Articles on Formatting. These tips could help you decide if DIY from scratch is for you. I could regurgitate it all here, but pointing you to this resource is, I believe, more comprehensive and helpful to you.

Also, I've been told that Scrivener makes formatting easy, but again, I haven't tried it yet.

Pro tips

Don't go tiny on your font to save paper or lower printing costs. Readers will hate you for it. And don't get all fancy with a font that's hard to read. Pick an old-style font and stay away from hard-to-read Times New Roman and Arial (or any sans serif font). Good ones? Garamond, Caslon, Minion, Janson Text, and Palatino. A handy article about fonts that will steer you right? "Picking Fonts for Your Indie Book," by Joel Friedlander (https://www.createspace.com/en/community/docs/DOC-1901). This article is also handy as a sleep aid.

My total expenditure on formatting was $39.50—the cost of Book Design Wizard. But my investment of time to format five nonfiction books for all of these venues as a first-timer? Two weeks. How long it will take me to do *Loser?* Three hours. How long it took me to do my first novel? Two hours. My second? One and a half. To me, that says that if you only have one or two books in you, especially if they're nonfiction, hire your formatting out unless you already have mad Word skillz.

Lock it down

Your last step will be to lock in your formatting by saving the files as PDFs—or to make sure your formatter did it for you. Yeah, yeah, you could upload to CreateSpace as a Word doc, but you can never guarantee that everything will look exactly as planned unless you set it in stone, and that's what PDFs do.

My little trick for doing this on the cheap, because Adobe software isn't: I downloaded Nitro PDF's Primo, which is free (http://primopdf.com). There are lots of other free PDF software applications; be sure to check out customer ratings before you download one, and always have a comprehensive internet security program running. I use AVG (http://avg.com). I also swear by their PC TuneUp to keep my laptop running efficiently, but I digress, and this is not a commercial for AVG. Back to your PDF.

When you set up the PDF, be sure that you change the page size of the document you are creating to match the page size of your book, and to embed your fonts and images. I found "Creating a PDF for Print" on CreateSpace very helpful (https://www.createspace.com/en/community/docs/DOC-1331).

Whatever method you choose for designing your book's interior, remember that the return on complexity diminishes rapidly for most books, and in some cases even works against you. Some readers want to focus on the words you wrote, not your hip style choices. Go figure.

23 • ROCK THE BLING AND SWAG

Increasing the visibility of your book's brand with promotional items

I'd hate to see you blow your budget on a bunch of worthless promotional crap, but I'd love to see you increase the visibility of your brand with some carefully chosen, cost-effective items. Plus, if you are going to hold events, or if you are going to sell books either directly or by consignment, you need to consider stocking a few goodies to hand out.

I adore Vistaprint (http://vistaprint.com) for inexpensive promotional items. I buy business cards with my cover on one side in full color and my print message in black and white on the back. I paid about $30 for 500 of them and I pass them out to every warm-blooded human I can. We've also experimented with Vistaprint's stickers , pens, bumper stickers, mugs, t-shirts, and even car magnets. I won't say you need all of those items, but my husband loves them (!!) and they make great gifts for volunteers, supporters, fans, and even family.

For inexpensive bookmarks, I use Printrunner (http://printrunner.com). I put a full-color slice of my cover on one side and black-and-white text on the other. They cost about $67 for 500, or 13.5¢ apiece, which is roughly half what CreateSpace charges.

We like to put up posters on community bulletin boards in libraries and grocery stores two to three weeks before book events. Sometimes we order 16x20-inch photo-quality reusable posters from Adorama Pix (http://adoramapix.com) for $10. Most of the time, though, we create one-use posters, and I've found I can go online to FedEx (http://fedex.com) and order 11x17 full-color copies for less than $2. You can get these through CreateSpace, too, but you order in batches of one hundred and they cost more than $2 each—and they are all identical. We also ordered book-cover prints from Adorama Pix that are suitable for signing for the avid fans who want to frame and display such an item. Don't buy these by the gross, for sure.

At events, I like to display my books on Lexan book stands. They're like little clear-plastic easels, and sometimes bookstores have them, too. When I give a speech and set up a table with my books on my little Lexans, it draws people in a way that flat stacks of books just can't. You can get them for about $3 each, and I've found them at Clear Displays (http://cleardisplays.com), Display Warehouse (http://displaywarehouse.com), and on Amazon (http://www.amazon.com/Amazon-6-pack-Acrylic-Easel-Holder/dp/B002Z6CJ9W).

Finally, if you want to display your books in an eye-catching way for consignment sales or to stand out at artisan fairs, craft shows, book festivals, and the like, big cardboard floor stands are surprisingly cheap and effective. You can get them for about $30 at Book Displays (http://bookdisplays.com).

For all of these items, allow three weeks so you can choose cheap shipping. Remember, too, that if you are working with a digital artist to create any of these items, you need to give her several weeks as well. If you are using your book cover and your portrait (did I mention you need a good high-resolution picture of yourself?) as your primary images, each of these items should take less than an hour for her to put together.

Anything else you buy should be because it makes you happy to own it or give it away, as very few other tchotchkes and hoohas make financial sense. But if owning a chef's hat with your book cover on it spices up your life, why not?

PART FIVE:
HOW TO PLAY IT FAST & LOOSE.

24 • PLAN TO BE POPULAR

You need to prepare a stand-alone marketing plan.

By now, you will have guessed that I believe in realistic budgeting and timelines and in working from a plan. I mentioned earlier that in my vision of an indie-publishing business plan, the marketing plan is a plan unto itself. It's that important, and that comprehensive, and that scary. It's the element writers fear most—it's so *extroverted*, so non-writerly, so *public*. Yet, if we want to sell books, we must do it. If we want to do it well, we must learn about it and plan for it.

Many of you have had zero experience with marketing books, and that's OK. I've got your back, and you'll be like a fish in water when I'm through with you. Well, maybe like a toddler with water wings. But you'll be afloat, and you'll learn to swim. It just takes practice.

To me, plans evolve from well-developed strategies. If you haven't figured out your sales strategy or put together your business plan, don't dive into the deep end yet with promotion plans. Work on first things first, but don't stop until you get here.

The elements of a marketing plan

1. Book information (including its price and expected or intended audience)

2. Book description

3. Author biography

4. Facets of the promotion you have planned for the book

If you're using your plan to entice potential booksellers, like we did, include a cover letter that tells them specifically what you are asking them to do and why they should do it.

Case study: My plan for *Saving Grace*

I'm feeling generous, so I'm going to attach a copy of the Marketing and Promotion Plan for my novel *Saving Grace* as an appendix to *Loser*. This is the same one we submitted to Barnes and Noble's Small Press Department. It cleared that hurdle and was sent on to the fiction buyer, who ordered the novel regionally and gave it a start. We sent a modified plan to Hastings Entertainment, and they ordered for all their stores. I'm not saying it's perfect, by any means, but it worked. If you want to download it, use these links:

Cover letter to Barnes and Noble Small Press Department: https://www.box.com/s/c57j7vvsvw6mhfhckezn

Marketing plan for *Saving Grace* presented to Barnes and Noble Small Press Department: https://www.box.com/s/4j3q4zmrojtjwyywykk9

The next few chapters will explore different ways to market and promote your book. You won't include all of these methods in your plan unless you're a nutjob like me. There's only so much money in your pocket and the day is limited to twenty-four hours. It's OK, too, to admit that some activities are too far outside your comfort zone and skill set. However, only by learning about each of them can you decide which ones will work for you. Then you can plan for them, budget for them, and stick them into your timeline. Heck, you might as well even do them, at that point. And they just might work.

25 • HELP ME HELP YOU

Become an active part of a community to raise visibility.

Writing a great book with wonderful cover art and getting it onto shelves, whether virtual or pine, is not enough to make it sell. Remember the boom in home-based internet businesses, when people thought all they needed to do was create a cool product and a website with a Buy button, and customers would flock to their sites and make them rich? Well, four or five of those companies made it, and the other three million are still having garage sales to try to get rid of all the doggie diapers and stained-glass window decorations they stockpiled.

Shouting "Buy my book!" over and over is not enough to make it sell, either, whether you do it online or in person. The only person who will buy it because you tell her to is your mother. Maybe. The rest of us? We'll just put our hands over our ears. Or unfollow you on Facebook. It's self-serving and annoying. You have no credibility with us. You give us no motivation to buy it just by telling us to. In fact, it motivates us to do exactly the opposite. People are peculiar that way.

So how does an indie-published author sell a book? By a multitude of simultaneous efforts in different venues to raise visibility—mostly by other people.

How to get visible

Since the question I get most often about promotion is "Can't someone else just do it for me?," I know some of you just cheered. Don't get too excited yet. You still play a major role in this drama.

Introduce yourself.

The first rule of visibility is this: Don't hide your light under a bushel basket. A lot of authors feel awkward about promoting their work. Well, stop that. Be proud of it! That doesn't mean shout "Buy my book." See above. It just doesn't work. But you should make sure people see your cover, hear your title, and read about your book—preferably, though, from people other than you.

Play well with others.

To do this, you need to build, join, or affiliate with a community of people with whom you have genuine and reciprocal relationships—even if you've never met them face-to-face—and gently cash in on all the nice things you've done for them. *They* raise your book's visibility for you.

Get a reputation.

Do you remember the phenomenon that was Paris Hilton? She was famous simply for being famous. She and her handlers had an incredible ability to get her face into every magazine, TV show, and newspaper. The general public assumed she was important because of how often it saw her, not because of anything she had actually done. She didn't ask the public to make her famous. She became famous because of her visibility, and because other people talked about her.

Try to make your book a classier version of Paris Hilton. The more your community talks about or links to your book, the more other people will see your cover and title, and thus—hopefully—the better it will sell. Books sell because people think they are selling. People think they are selling because other people talk about them. Does that make sense?

How to get popular

Once you've built a community of real people enjoying genuine and reciprocal relationships, you need to get them talking about your book.

Give your friends presents.

One of the best ways to raise your book's visibility within your community is to give it away. While this might seem counter to the goal of making money, it is one of the best ways to get people to read, talk about, and recommend your book. Visibility is about buzz, and buzz doesn't start by itself. If you're asking your community to start buzzing for you, doesn't it make sense that you'd do something for them first? Give them the dang book, people. E-mail them a PDF file. It won't cost you a cent, and they just might buzz like crazy. This is grassroots marketing at its finest.

Give strangers presents, too.

Keep a marketing box stocked with bookmarks, cards, fliers, and paperbacks (which you know I think you should have). Mark the books "Lobby Copy" and tape your business card inside, and maybe even write "Available on Amazon" on the title page. Drop them around town in waiting areas at doctors' offices, barber shops, hair salons, and spas. Anywhere there are chairs and tables with magazines. Leave bookmarks on tables. That big public bulletin board at the grocery store? Put up your flyer. That store that allows people to leave a stack of business cards? Leave yours—the one with your book cover on it.

Will these things on their own sell books? Probably not. But the point is visibility. People rarely purchase a book from a new author the first time they see the cover. However, if they see it while waiting for the doctor, and then see it again on a poster while walking into the grocery store, and then see it again when they get their hair done, some of them begin to think, "Wow, I've seen that book *everywhere*, this book must be popular, this book must be selling, I should get one."

When you're plagued with self-doubt

If something negative inside you rears its head and says, "I am only one little person in one little town. How can these things really help me?," I have three responses:

—If you do nothing, I can do the math on your sales figures for you.

—You have to start somewhere, and book sales beget more books sales. If your book is good, and if you are able to get ten people to actually read it, they may each tell ten more people who become potential customers, who may each tell ten more, and so on. Do *that* math.

—Turn to your community. See if some of them are willing to do this same thing for you in their cities. And *return those favors* by doing what you can for them in yours for their causes and enterprises.

Is promoting your own books easy? No. Is it possible? Yes. Is it hard? Yes, but even though it's hard, it's pretty dang fun. And to make it easier and even more fun, I've included my "How to Help an Indie Author" flier as an appendix to this book. You can use it and my Grassroots Army spreadsheet to help you rally your troops.

26 • MAKE YOURSELF STALKABLE

An author must have a website. Here's how to build one.

If you're going to sell books, you have to have a website. Period. Readers need a place to land to read about you and your books. It's your online brochure. It toots your horn. It propels browsers to purchase and points them to where.

Good news, though: it doesn't have to cost a lot of money, be fancy, or require soul-crushing hours of upkeep. If you *want* a fancy, expensive, high-maintenance website, knock yourself out. In that case, you've got this chapter wired and can give it a brief skim. I'm talking to the rest of you, the ones who fear development of your own website like a plague of locusts. Or a zombie apocalypse. Or getting a run in your hose right before you deliver a pitch to an editor from Random House.

Your website can be static or you can update its content regularly. A static website's pages mostly stay the same, and websites with frequently updated content often feature a blog or a news ticker. I'll speak to each, but first let's talk about how a website is built.

The easiest way: pay someone.

You can ask a web designer to do something simple and clean that requires little maintenance. Offer links to author websites you like as examples. Draft the copy for the types of pages you want and give it to the designer with images and photos for him to use. You should expect an interactive process that takes several months.

To find a good web designer, ask for referrals from your local writing group and Google (you knew I was going to say that, didn't you?) for book- or author-website designers. Many author-service providers offer website development, as well. When you find someone, ask for links to sites they have designed and for contact information for a few of their clients, preferably the ones for whom they did the websites they offer as samples. Contact the clients and find out whether they were satisfied with the designer's services, including quality, pace, price, and communication.

Expect to pay between $35 and $100 an hour. If you're quoted a flat fee, ask what it's based on. Get samples, references, and quotes from several designers for comparison. Work with someone you feel will make the process less than torturous for you.

Domain names

You will have a choice of whether to use a free or paid domain name. (The domain name is the last part of a web address, i.e., wikipedia.com or tamu.edu.) Free domain names usually have the web company's name in them: hotshotauthor.blogspot.com, hotshotauthor.wordpress.com. Paid domain names do not, as in hotshotauthor.com. Whichever you pick, try to brand either your name or book with this choice. Of these two, your author name will give you more versatility in the long run, and I highly recommend it.

For instance, the URL (complete address) for my website is http://pamelahutchins.com. I am branding my name. If I had it to do over again, I'd choose pamelafaganhutchins.com, but at the time I worried that lazy surfers wouldn't want to type all those extra letters. I made the same error on Facebook, by the way. But then I'm not claiming to be perfect. It's like my parents always told me, "Do as I say, not as I do."

I bought my domain name from GoDaddy (http://godaddy.com). While I am not a big fan of their Super Bowl ads, their prices are low and their customer service is good. You pay an annual fee of around $100, including web hosting. Sometimes more.

Paying for your domain name will give you access to e-mail addresses that match it, hence my pamela@pamelahutchins.com. Again, it captures a brand, and it makes it easy for your readers to send you fan mail. Hey, I do get some now and then, really! GoDaddy's site led me through instructions for my e-mail, but it isn't for the fainthearted. A web designer can help you with this, as well.

A custom domain name and matching e-mail address is a mark of professionalism that will set you apart and help you as you strive for publishing legitimacy; they're your online business cards. Having a Blogspot URL or Gmail address for your publishing business is like scribbling down your phone number on a restaurant napkin. A permanent domain name sends the message that you're here to stay.

Blogging

If you envision more than a static web page, your best and easiest bet is to set up a blog that runs either on your home (landing) page or one of the other pages on your website. A designer can set this up for you. I believe in the community-assembling power of blogging, and I talked about some of the benefits of community earlier in *Loser*. A blog is a wonderful way to build a following. You can interact with readers via comments. It allows you to test-market your writing almost instantaneously. If you're disciplined and set yourself up with an editorial calendar, you can multitask by creating posts you'll later use for books.

Blogging keeps your website fresh with new content, which raises your visibility with search engines. You can go even further with targeted search engine optimization (SEO). Your web designer can help you with that, or you can do it yourself, if you're a brainiac.

I use a WordPress (http://wordpress.com) blogging platform. I used to use Google's Blogger (http://blogger.com), but I migrated to WordPress and like it better. Both are fine. There are others. I liked WordPress so much that when it came time to upgrade my blog to a real website with a custom URL, I purchased a WordPress template to use with my GoDaddy site.

WordPress (and Blogger, too) has tons of widgets and free plug-ins, which are apps you can install to make your simple little website do really cool things. Not all plug-ins are free, but what you decide to spend your coin on is up to you. I installed plug-ins that do things like insert social-media links, add a news ticker, insert standard copy at the bottom of each blog post, suggest related posts, and control spam comments, to name just a few. If you have a designer, talk to him about the features you'd like on your website, and suggest to him you'd like to use free plug-ins to keep your costs down.

Confession: I secretly obtained a computer-science-type degree as an undergrad, so I do my own website, albeit not very well, since I abandoned geekhood for law school immediately upon graduation. If you have even a modicum of tech savvy, you can probably muddle through the instructions available online. But it is no shame to hire someone to do it for you, and in fact might be cost effective if you have a few hundred dollars to spare and other valuable activities competing for your time.

What should you blog?

If you decide to blog, write about topics that will interest your desired audience. This is one of the best ways to grow your platform. Did you write a book about Vietnamese refugees? Then write about Vietnamese food, history, or culture. Is your book a thriller in Nepal? Write about mountain climbing or adventure travel. You can also blog book reviews in your genre. Write about whatever you want to, but you'll get the most mileage from it if it interests the audience you want to attract. Publish it regularly, say once or twice a week, and keep your posts about 300–800 words long (that equates to 1–3 double-spaced pages in Word).

Why should you blog?

You're angling for the holiest of holies: subscription. You want your readers to hang on your every post and thus to subscribe by e-mail (the holy grail) or RSS feed. RSS stands for Really Simple Syndication, and is a process that delivers content to readers' feeders, like Digg (http://digg.com), Feedly (http://feedly.com), Bloglines (http://bloglines.com), NewsBlur (http://newsblur.com), and many more. You don't have to understand how to use feed readers, you just need to know that they help readers receive and read your blog posts, and that they are your friends. Don't waste any hits on your website. Offer a chance for visitors not only to subscribe to your blog but also to join your new-release mailing list. I'll talk about this more soon.

Who will read your blog?

To attract readers, tell everyone you know that you've started a blog, and invite them to read and comment on it. Don't beat them over the head about it repeatedly. One e-mail will do. Those who are interested will bite. Those who aren't won't, and they are not (necessarily) evil people.

Your next step will be to engage in social media and post links to your blog that are interesting and non-spammy. This may

145

freak the tube socks right off your feet, even over your desperately curling toes. Take a deep cleansing breath through a brown paper bag. Your anxiety will lessen somewhat over time.

Another great way to attract readers is to visit blogs that interest you and comment on posts in interesting and insightful ways, making sure to include the web address of your own blog. With luck, your blog readers will become contacts who later read your books—and maybe even pay money for your books.

I've found that my subscribers and commenters turn into friends and supporters, people who do nice things for me and for whom I do nice things as well. Community, in other words. Some of them are my beta readers. Many of them have reviewed my books. All of them I hope dearly to meet in real life (IRL) someday, maybe at a book event or when their travel brings them to my stomping grounds.

Once you have a website, don't be shy. Include your web address in your bios, on your business cards, and in your social-media contact information. Make it easy for people to stalk you, then spin them into the web of words you have built. After all, that's what you want, isn't it? For people to not be able to get enough of you? Open the door and invite them in, and make sure you've got the feast ready when they get there.

27 • LET THEM TALK

How to obtain critically important reviews of your book

I cannot stress enough the importance of book reviews to sales of indie-published books. The question is, without big publishing behind you, how do you get them? It's not like the *New York Times'* book editor is counting the days until your book arrives.

The easy way? Pay for them.

One school of thought is to buy them. There are certainly many sources for paid reviews, some of which reach a very large audience and are quite credible. There is another school of thought that says you should never buy them. My thought: you should never buy them from individuals, because it calls the reviewers' credibility into question. But I don't think there's anything wrong with buying them from the same sources that publishing companies do.

Wait! That's blasphemy!! Pamela is going to hell!! Publishing companies don't pay for reviews!!

Or do they? How do literary periodicals stay in business, if not for the money spent by publishers? When a major house buys a huge block of advertising from a literary publication, do you think it comes with the expectation that their authors will receive reviews? I think you can bet your booty it does. And don't you think that if the major house doesn't get that from the publication, it will spend its money elsewhere? The major house is running a business, after all, a business that needs reviews for its authors.

I believe the only way to level that playing field is for the indie author to spend money with those credible industry-review sources. Period. Keep in mind, you're not paying for a *good* review. You're paying for a credible review, and it may be scathing. That's the chance you take.

Kirkus Indie (http://kirkusreviews.com/indie/about/), for example, reviews indie books for $425. They require a good bit of lead time (7–9 weeks) for this price. They expedite (3–4 weeks) for $575. It doesn't carry quite the panache of Kirkus for the non-indie world, but it's still very, very solid.

Yet pricey.

You can ask them not to publish it if the review comes back unfavorable. If you do authorize them to publish it on their website, they will push it to their partners, including BarnesandNoble.com. They may even choose to publish it in *Kirkus Reviews*, their main publication. If they do, you should buy a bottle of champagne—Dom Perignon, not Cook's. You've just won the indie-publishing review lottery.

Publishers Weekly has an indie "promotion" service, too, through their PW Select (http://www.publishersweekly.com/pw/diy/index.html). At $125, it's cheaper than Kirkus Indie, but they don't guarantee they'll review your book, only that they'll include it in their PW Select insert in *Publisher's Weekly*. They claim to review about 25% of their submissions, but they certainly won't if you don't get PW Select.

The hard way: ask for them.

Periodicals

There are lots of ways for indie authors to get free reviews. One is to solicit them from newspapers and periodicals directly. Why not shoot for the *New York Times?* Just be sure you do it four months before your book comes out so you have a prayer of them getting to it. A great resource for finding reviewers is John Kremer's Book Market website, and specifically his Publicity Resources page (http://www.bookmarket.com/publicity.htm). Choose a target, then write a nice cover letter and stick it and your press release into a paperback copy of your book (yes, a hard copy), sprinkle pixie dust over it, and seal it with a kiss. Sometimes you'll have more success with a newspaper reviewer in a particular city if you are holding an event there. This has worked for me on several occasions.

Book bloggers

Reviews from book bloggers can really help a book find its wings. One way to get in front of them is to book a blog tour. The blog tour organizer sends your book out to book bloggers who review in your genre, and gets you on their schedule. Blog tours are not free. I use Pump Up Your Book (http://pumpupyourbook.com), but there are many, many services available. Just Google "book blog tour" and browse to your heart's content. If the list is too unwieldy, maybe add your genre to the search to narrow your results. You should pay somewhere between $50 and $500 for a good, month-long tour with fifteen "stops." Ideally, you'll stop at blogs that get significant traffic; pricing for different tours is often based on this anticipated traffic. You will find services that charge more than $500 per month, but I sincerely doubt that spending more will be worth it for a new indie author. Book your tour several months in advance.

If you don't want to pay for a blog tour service—or if you can't find one that matches the type of book you've written—

you can solicit book blogger reviews on your own. But how to find the book bloggers? The Indie Book Reviewer (http://indiebookreview.blogspot.com) is a good source. Be sure that you approach the reviewers in the same way you would query an agent:

1. Go to their website. Are they open for submissions? Does your book fit their interests and genre?

2. Submit in the form specified on their website.

3. Describe your book in a compelling manner, as you would in a pitch or query to an agent. There are good examples of how (and how not) to do that at The Query Shark (http://queryshark.blogspot.com).

4. If a reviewer says yes, get the (free) book to them in the format requested, then work to promote the heck out of their review site upon publication. They've scratched your back. Now scratch theirs. Even if you don't like the review, it is press, and all press is good press. Don't forget to ask them to post some or all of it on Amazon and Goodreads.

5. Never, ever, ever pay one of these reviewers. Kirkus, yes. Indie reviewers, no. (Note: giving someone a book for the purpose of a review is not paying them—it's the least you can do since you're asking for them to do something for you.)

One review is not enough. Solicit as many as you can. To maximize the buzz, try your best to time them so they all come out in a two-to-four-week window. However, you can't dictate reviewers' schedules any more than you can dictate what they write. Best to start three months in advance and sweetly suggest a time frame that is optimal. They're likely to work with you if you've given them adequate notice.

Expect some book bloggers to have alternate vehicles for exposure, like author interviews or guest posts. Say yes if they offer, even if they say no to reviewing your book. Some like to have you do a giveaway in conjunction with their review. Say yes, as it increases readership of the review. Some like to do a cover reveal for you. It's a good idea, so think about it. Expect to get eight no's for every ten requests you send out. These indie book bloggers are busy, too, like you.

Friends and "friends"

Another way an indie author can get reviews is to invite social-media contacts to write and post reviews on their blogs or in other social-media venues. Again, don't forget to have them post some or all of the reviews on Amazon and Goodreads. Your reviewers will be amateurs and the exposure you gain may be limited, but they are still raising awareness for you. Offer to return a similar favor to them. Maybe they don't want to review your book, but they'll allow you to post an excerpt or do an interview or guest post. Say yes. Then promote the heck out of it.

And of course there are always the straight-to-Amazon and straight-to-Goodreads reviews that you should constantly work toward getting posted. Ask anyone you know who reads your book to post one. Then remind them. Then bribe them. Whatever it takes! I'm only *partially* kidding on the bribery— but book giveaways, while not bribery, are a great way to incentivize the behavior of posting reviews.

Don't be surprised when it's as hard to get your best friend to post a review on Amazon and Goodreads as it is to get one from the *New York Times*. It's damn hard to get your contacts to post reviews for your books. I get it. I never posted a review unless asked until I published my first book. Now I'm a review-posting fool. I post honestly, but I never post mean or personally insulting reviews.

It's like pulling teeth for the tooth fairy

Want to read more on this important topic? I recommend "How to Get Your Book Reviewed" (http://www.molly-greene.com/how-to-get-your-book-reviewed/), by Christine Nolfi, on the blog of writer Molly Greene.

Let's get real: you may not get any reviews from any of these ideas. And who's going to give you your first five? I'll bet your mom, spouse, and twin sibling are on the list. Every time I read reviews of an indie book, I see this. I'm amused by it, but I've lived it. It takes a lot of sparks to start a fire, and we use any flints we can.

For many authors, the reviews stop after this inner circle finishes posting. If you're energetic, persuasive, and strategic (in other words, if you spam everyone you know until they give in out of desperation to MAKE IT STOP—*just kidding*), you can keep building on that initial flicker until you get a nice little flame.

Reviews not only beget sales which beget rankings which beget more sales, but reviews on Amazon are sometimes the ante-up to promotion *by Amazon*. I launched *Saving Grace* on Amazon with free days through KDP Select, employing some very inexpensive advertising to promote my giveaway (which I'll address in a later chapter), and ended up after four days at #1 in free downloads out of 55,000+ books per day. My book was downloaded by 33,016 people, and some of them even read it. I was elated, and this propelled me into big sales over the next month.

But none of this would have happened without reviews. Why? Because the websites I paid for promotion wouldn't even take my money unless I had more than fifteen reviews and an average of at least 4 out of 5 stars. It's their way of ensuring they don't promote crap to their readership. I applaud them for it, but it is a tough hurdle to cross.

Conventional wisdom says you'll give away 200–500 free books in hopes of reviews (yes, I just said 200–500, but that can include PDF copies and e-books), but hardly any of those people will end up reviewing it. Not by a long shot.

When the tooth fairy turns on you

So here's where a little-read Amazon review policy comes into play in a nasty way. It's the policy you'd probably only learn about if you noticed Amazon pulling your book's reviews down—*and* if you had the intestinal fortitude to challenge them on it (via a Contact Us button, because you're not allowed to talk to them IRL) despite any trepidation you had as you simultaneously snarfed up sales out of their hand.

Let's start with a review by a spouse. My husband posted reviews on my books. Eric is uber-supportive. And cute, too. His reviews were yanked. He contacted Amazon. They said:

We have removed your reviews as we do not allow reviews on behalf of a person or company with a financial interest in the product or a directly competing product. This includes **authors, artists, publishers, manufacturers, or third-party merchants selling the product (emphasis added)**. *As a result, we've removed your reviews for this title. Any further violations of our posted Guidelines may result in the removal of this item from our website.*

Ouchy. Scary, that last sentence. Now, they did not say spouses. But since we are married, we decided not to push it. When I lose money, Eric loses money. So it stands to reason he would profit if I ever did.

My mother posted reviews. Her last name matches my middle name/maiden name, Fagan. Amazon yanked them down. My uncle, last name of Fagan and himself a writer, posted a review. Amazon yanked it. My adult stepdaughter living in Colorado posted a review; Hutchins is her last name. Amazon pulled it. Eric complained, and so did my mother and my uncle. Amazon responded (and by now Eric and Amazon were on a first-name basis):

I understand your concerns about these missing reviews by other members of Pamela's family. We take the removal of customer reviews very seriously.

I'm not able to tell you why these specific reviews were removed from our website. I can only discuss that with the person who wrote each review. However, I can tell you that reviews are removed from the Amazon.com website for three reasons:

1. The review conflicted with our posted guidelines http://www.amazon.com/review-guidelines/.

2. The review was removed at the request of the customer who submitted the review.

3. We discovered that multiple items were linked together on our website incorrectly. Reviews that were posted on those pages were removed when the items were separated on the site.

Thank you for your understanding of our policies, Eric. We look forward to seeing you again soon and have a good day.

The referenced review policy prohibited, amongst other things:

Promotional content:

• Sentiments by or on behalf of a person or company with a financial interest in the product or a directly competing product (including reviews by publishers, manufacturers, or third-party merchants selling the product)

All involved assured Amazon that this was not the case. And it wasn't. I can promise you, none of the listed individuals has volunteered to share in our household tax write-off, a.k.a. Pamela's writing career. Amazon was not able to state a valid reason for sucking my mother's and uncle's reviews into a black hole, and they encouraged them to repost.

They gobbled up the reposts, too.

By this point, even our most loyal fans have had it, right? I mean, they are *done*. There are more enjoyable things to do with one's day than posting and reposting reviews, like scrubbing your grout with a toothbrush, or going in for that quadruple root canal you've put off for six months.

Maybe there are better people in the world to post reviews than family, too—well, undoubtedly there are—but my point is this: Amazon is not allowing legitimate reviewers who are permissible under their own policy to review books.

For me, it didn't stop there.

After Amazon decided to blackball my stepdaughter, mother, and uncle, they went on to blackball anyone with the name Pamela, Hutchins, or Fagan, or that had any connection to us. From what we could tell, that included IP addresses, which knocked out the results from my little "here's how to review a book" party, which I had thought was a damn good idea. They yanked reviews by reviewers I've never met. All of these were, per Amazon's own policy, legitimate reviews, from what I could tell from the ones sent to me.

And they're gone. It's not like Amazon kindly reinstates them once you raise it to their attention. You have to try again. But we've seen over and over what happens when you do: Amazon gobbles them up like a big meanie.

This hits authors in the pocket. Reviews beget sales beget rankings beget more sales. And it's cyclical, since reviews beget more reviews. Many people seem to feel safer leaving a review in an anonymous crowd.

I think this review gobbler on Amazon has gone overboard. Save my blood pressure: sign this petition to ask Amazon to stop arbitrarily removing customer reviews from indie books (http://www.change.org/petitions/amazon-stop-arbitrarily-removing-customer-reviews-from-indie-author-books).

Taking a step back for perspective, Amazon has made it possible for indie authors to sell their books. I am an indie author. I am selling a lot of books on Amazon, and I am grateful. But how much more could authors make if legitimate reviews were not overzealously pulled from their books? We don't have the might of Penguin, who can call up an Amazon executive when one of its authors loses reviews and say "WTF, Jeff?"

Last words for the wise

—Do encourage *honest* reviews

—Don't review your own book (although you can rate your own book on Goodreads)

—Don't pay for book bloggers or individuals to review your book

—Don't *ever* respond to a review online, even if it is wrong or personally insulting—you take the high road. If you don't, you run the risk of a flaming epic online battle that you *will* lose in the court of public opinion. Trust me.

28 • GIVE IT AWAY

Giveaways beget goodwill (and book sales).

I've been saying it, and now I'm going to say it some more: you're going to have to give away some books. This hurts some of you. In the last chapter, I talked about giving away hundreds, and I know that's not just pain, it's torture. It's also optional.

One of the main reasons for going indie is the right to call your own shots. You get to decide how many books you want to give away. Maybe it won't be several hundred. Maybe you only plan to write one book in your entire life, so you're not concerned about building readership for your future publications. Maybe you just want to see what you can make from this one book, and you don't believe in giving away something you labored over for ten years.

I hear you. I abhorred the idea of giving my books away when I first published. My husband had owned an indie bookstore, though, and he was way more savvy than me.

"You're trying to build readers, Pamela, readers for your future books," Eric said.

"Yeah, readers that pay for my books," I said.

"People buy books because other people buy books. They buy them because of word of mouth, reviews, and sales rankings. They buy them because they see your cover five times and suddenly believe it's good, even though they've never heard a word about it."

"And your point is?"

"You have to start somewhere. You need those first one hundred people to review, carry around, and talk about your books. You need to give them books."

I didn't give in right away. But when I did try a Goodreads giveaway, you know what I found out? The people who won my books reviewed them. (I asked them to, very nicely, when I shipped the books to them.) And I added that the reviews should be honest. I adhere to the "If you hate it, it's OK to state it" approach. Luckily there have been very few haters out there. Those Goodreads reviews attracted attention and created buzz, which led to sales.

I did giveaways on my website. By the way, I love me some Rafflecopter for giveaways (http://rafflecopter.com). It's completely free, keeps track of entries, and allows you to set requirements for entrants, like that they follow you on Facebook or Twitter, for instance. Anyway, the Rafflecopter giveaways generated traffic to my website and reviews, which created buzz, which led to sales.

OK, I was beginning to see Eric's logic.

So we decided to experiment with KDP Select's free days, which I touched on in the last chapter.

The year KDP Select rocked my world

For those who are skipping around in *Loser*, KDP Select is an Amazon promotion that (among other things) lets authors give away e-books for free for up to five days of a ninety-day period in which the title is sold exclusively through Amazon. This allows authors to reach some new readers who may purchase their books in the future. In the meantime, it drives up the book's ranking on Amazon's lists of best sellers, both overall and in specific categories, and in Hot New Releases, if it's within the book's first thirty days. Another benefit is that authors share a piece of the Amazon Prime pie as part of KOLL (Kindle's lending library).

KDP Select's exclusivity deal does not extend to physical or audio books, so an author can still sell everything but e-books anywhere and everywhere.

To read a great article discussing KDP Select and promotions, I recommend David Gaughran's "Popularity, Visibility, & KDP Select" (http://davidgaughran.wordpress.com/2012/10/22/popularity-visibility-kdp-select/). To see what Amazon has to say, visit its KDP Select page (https://kdp.amazon.com/self-publishing/KDPSelect).

I can't pretend to understand (yet) all the Amazon algorithms for Best Sellers, Hot New Releases, and popularity, but I do know that my combined sales from other e-book sales outlets weren't enough to keep us from experimenting with KDP Select. Especially since, at that time, I had six titles. Why was the multi-title aspect important to me? Because each promotion period on each book hopefully would impact sales of the other books positively. It's a multiplier, if you will. Meanwhile, our goal is long-term sellability for each book, so giving away my books now to increase sales later was making more and more sense to me. Eric and I think of my writing and our publishing as an investment in our retirement, not as a "quit the day job" endeavor. If it exceeds our expectations, we'll be happily surprised.

In October of 2012, I released my debut novel, *Saving Grace*, via a free Kindle promo on Amazon using KDP Select. Five days later, I'd had a twenty-four-hour run as the #1 free download on Amazon with over 33,000 downloads. It went fairly well, to say the least. It exceeded my goals by about 23,000 downloads, in fact, and I shed tears when I broke the top 100. Yes, I really did. The rest was just the best gravy ever.

It didn't stop there, though. In the two weeks after the free promo, *Saving Grace* moved to #10 in women sleuths and #30 in women's fiction, peaking at #390 overall on Amazon—in *paid* downloads. I was featured as Top Rated on the women sleuths page. The best thing about the post-free-promo days was Kindle Prime, which enabled hordes of people to download *Saving Grace* on loan. Each loan counted toward my paid downloads and sales and helped me stay high in the rankings.

My review count went from nineteen to fifty-two during this period and I held onto a 4.5-star rating. The more books I gave away, the more money I made, the more visibility my name and my book gained, and the more reviews people left on Amazon for my book. It was all kinds of awesome.

Keep in mind that your KDP Select free days generate only Amazon reviews. Goodreads is a different audience, and if you want to generate reviews there, you should consider running giveaways there. By the way, Goodreads requires you to mail hard copies to the winners. A word about giving away downloads to my friends-and-family platform folks—possibly the only people that would have paid for my book, had I not done the free promo:

1. They cared enough to leave reviews; most people don't.

2. Getting the book for free gave them a reason to create buzz with their friends and family. Buzz is good.

3. The time constraints of the free days created an urgency that got them to read the book sooner rather than later. This sped up the buzz and concentrated it.

4. It is my sincere belief that these are the folks who will buy the paperback version anyway and give it as a gift.

I worried about giving away books before my promo, but I never will again.

How to do KDP Select right

"Hot damn," you're thinking. "She's going to give me an easy, free formula to guarantee my success."

Sorry, friends. Ain't gonna happen. I'm going to give you a formula, all right, but here's the truth: you probably already know 90% of what you need to know to position your book for a great KDP Select run. I'll share another 7%, and 3% is up to fate, in my humble opinion.

First though, what is a great run? It depends on your book. If it doesn't have the potential for widespread appeal, then keep your goals modest. My dynamite little relationship book, *How to Screw Up Your Marriage: Do-Over Tips for First-Time Failures*, did less than 400 downloads in its three free promo days, but it went to #1 in Divorce and #1 in Marriage, and I was delighted. Those audiences are much, much smaller. But 75% of all books (in any format) are purchased by women over forty, or so I was told at a Writer's Digest Editor's Intensive Conference, so if your book appeals at all to that demographic, then you should set your download goals higher.

OK, now let's talk tips. Some of this should sound familiar.

1. Edit your book.

If your book isn't professionally edited, your success has a low ceiling. You didn't want to hear that, did you? But it's true. Can't afford an editor? Sell your car. Try crowdfunding. Barter services. Otherwise, wait until you have the money, or go the traditional route. Top-notch editing is not optional for a successful book. Amazon's previews let people open your book before they download it, and bad editing doesn't make the cut for a lot of people, even in a free book.

I do love the books edited solely by your critique group, though. They make my editor look really good.

2. Get a great cover.

Again, spend the money on a professional who can make a grab-ya cover. See my suggestions in #1 for ways to raise money. My *Saving Grace* cover, designed by Heidi Dorey (who I plan to keep so busy she doesn't have time for anyone else), drove downloads. Weak covers don't. And they must convey their power in 100×150 pixels, which is a tremendous challenge.

3. Plan well ahead.

Start months ahead and plan promotion for a free run that will last at least three consecutive days. I did five, and I'm glad I did. Work in advance on that dirty word, PLATFORM (or call it community, network, or your peeps, whatever), so you have an audience to ask to drink your Kool-Aid to get your initial download bump.

Your planned promotion should be comprehensive. Consult Kindle Book Review's Author Resources page (http://www.thekindlebookreview.net/author-resources/) for options on free and low-to-medium-cost online promotion. Bookmark the page. Send KBR's Jeff Bennington a thank-you note. Set a budget. Schedule your dates two months in advance. Spend the money you budgeted. I spent $150 and made $1,000 in Kindle royalties on *Saving Grace* in the next week alone. I think it was worth it.

4. Look good online.

Be sure your author and book pages on Amazon are sparkly and tight. The value of your book must be clear; your author creds must be solid and interesting. And don't forget: emotion begets action. Create an exciting book page that plays on emotion. Carolyn McCray of the Indie Book Collective has some wise words on book pages, and I recommend her post on Digital Book World (http://www.digitalbookworld.com/2011/best-practices-for-amazon-ebook-sales/). For pointers on author pages, I like

Dana Lynn Smith's website, The Savvy Book Marketer (http://bookmarketingmaven.typepad.com/book_marketing_maven/optimizing_amazon/).

5. Raise your prices.

Seeing the difference between the stated price and "Free!" has a psychological impact that drives downloads.

6. Get good reviews.

In my opinion, you need twenty-five Amazon reviews of a 4-star rating or higher to get significant traction. Good luck. Start early. Follow Amazon's rules to the letter, and expect that some of your reviews will be arbitrarily pulled. [OK, I have to stop talking about this now, because my face is getting purple. Here's another plea to save my blood pressure: sign this petition to Amazon (http://www.change.org/petitions/amazon-stop-arbitrarily-removing-customer-reviews-from-indie-author-books).]

Reviews are everything

Reviews are everything

Reviews are everything

7. Layer your promotion.

Make your promotion multi-pronged, or layered, to reach multiple audiences through multiple sites. I relied on a few online resources to guide my free-promo strategy. The best of them: "Maximize Your KDP Select Days." (http://digitalbooktoday.com/maximize-your-kdp-select-free-days/) Google it. You'll find a ton more.

Why plan ahead, and why wait for reviews to be in place? Here's how it worked for me:

Day 1: My friends, family, and community, both IRL and online, took pity on me (or bowed to the pressure of my relentless Twitter and Facebook spamming, you tell me), and downloaded *Saving Grace* at a rate that still makes my heart soar. Thank you, everyone! You know who you are.

Day 2: My $40 one-day Social Media Buzz promo with Digital Book Today (http://digitalbooktoday.com/) began—in retrospect, a fantastic call. But I was only able to make the most of DBT because I had nineteen reviews, eighteen of which were 5-star. (This promotion now requires more than twenty-five reviews.) DBT featured *Saving Grace* on its website and its Facebook page, tweeted about it, and considered it for its The Best Free Kindle Books list. For me, this meant waking up on day two to see *Saving Grace* at #1 on DBT's list. Thank you, DBT's Anthony Wessel. Thank you, kind people with discerning literary taste who reviewed my book. *Saving Grace* took off like a rocket as soon as the list went up.

Day 3: My $45 one-day Social Media Mania promo with World Literary Cafe (http://worldliterarycafe.com/) took *Saving Grace* into overdrive. WLC included my book on its web page and Facebook pages and tweeted my giveaway like mad. The one-two punch of DBT's list and the tweeting frenzy of the WLC's Tweet Teams was staggering. And here's where I thank Melissa Foster: Thanks, Melissa!

Day 4: I did a $40 Twitterlicious promo with Kindle Book Review, and it kept the buzz alive on their website and through more tweets.

I also used Jeff Bennington's Author Resources on KBR to post *Saving Grace*'s free days on every free site I could find. And don't forget Amazon's international markets when you're building your layers. I tweeted links for the UK, Germany, France, Spain, Italy, and Japan on a daily basis, and scheduled them ahead of time through Tweetdeck. I did pretty darn well in the UK, too.

8. Engage people with your excitement.

When you reach a milestone, thank your supporters and share the news. I found that my supporters really wanted to share in the success that they rightly felt they'd contributed to. I did a lot of screenshot posts to Twitter and Facebook as I moved up in the rankings. This kept my best supporters buzzing like crazy.

9. Post-promo, let it go.

a. When it's done, let it be done. Don't wear out your welcome. Resume (see #10) promoting other people instead.

b. Drop your price! For better or worse, I chose to price the paperback version of *Saving Grace* at $4.99, down from $7.99 during the promo. Re-read my chapter on pricing strategy. You'll have to decide what price is right for your book.

c. Keep the buzz alive. I ran a Today's Hot Titles banner on World Literary Cafe in my first week post-promo for $25 per day. It was cheap. It helped. I tried the $99 Twitter Buzz with The Women's Nest (http://thewomensnest.com) the next week, and they tweeted for me and kept my buzz going somewhat, but without the World Literary Cafe Tweet Teams to keep the message moving, this paid promo did not have nearly as large an impact as WLC. I didn't plan far enough in advance to schedule promo with some great sites, like Kindle Nation Daily (http://kindlenationdaily.com), but I still seemed to do pretty well. And they're a little pricey, anyway.

10. Be gracious.

Every chance you get, say thank you, again and again and again and again, in part because it's the nice thing to do, and also because it inspires others to help you. Every time I thanked someone on Facebook or Twitter for pushing my promo or leaving a review, someone else offered to help. Can you say SNOWBALL?

Don't stop with thank you. Pay it forward. Help them, all of them, no matter how long it takes. And please note that the amount of effort you've expended promoting others *prior* to your free download will be directly related to the numbers that line up to help you *during* it. Invest in your community early and often, or they won't invest in you. This is how you move mountains in platform building (see #3).

29 • GAME THE COMPETITION

The value of writing contests and how to do them right

I love writing contests. I don't keep it much of a secret. As Garrett Morris used to say on *Saturday Night Live*, "Contests been veddy veddy good to me." Or something like that, anyway.

So the question isn't whether I'm a contest proponent, but why. Let me explain the whys, and if I convince you of their merit, stick around for a few whens, wheres, and hows.

Why they're worth it

1. Many contests (but not all!) provide a critique sheet. Before you publish that book, you need unbiased critical feedback. How good is your critique group? Can they really be unbiased? The contest critiquer can, and the critical analysis of your manuscript and its relative position against other contest entries is worth the price of admission, even if you don't win.

2. Many contests suffer from too few entries. Few have the opposite problem. So your chances to win, place, or show may be greater than you think.

3. Contests help writers get over the fear of submission and publication.

"Yegads," you say, "you mean I have to let someone else read my work and espouse their opinions?"

Jump in. The water's fine.

4. The judges may be agents or editors. Yes, this could be your big break. It probably won't be, but you've got a better chance than all the other schmucks who didn't submit.

5. You could win. Contest wins give your book credibility. They give you fodder for a press release. They help you sell books.

When to enter

Don't enter a book that isn't finished. Don't enter a book that isn't ready for submission.

Are you still with me? Good. Let's talk about how to find contests and which ones you should enter.

Where to find them

Local, regional, and national writing groups and conferences often hold annual competitions. Start in your region and genre by perusing websites and newsletters.

Looking for someone to do the heavy lifting for you? Here are a few good lists, but none are comprehensive:

—Writer's Digest
http://writersdigest.com/competitions/writing-competitions/

—Writers-Editors

http://writers-editors.com/writers/contests/contests.htm

—Poets & Writers
http://www.pw.org/content/writing_contests_0

Just Google "writing contests" and the genre and year. You'll get lots of choices. Pick contests that suit your work, of course, and don't be afraid to e-mail the organizer and ask how many entries they anticipate. If your writing is not yet contest-tested, start small and work your way up to bigger competitions.

How to enter

Most contests list confusing explicit instructions. Entry may require any of the following:

1. Entry fee: The higher the award, the higher the fee. Expect around $50. There's often a discount for multiple entries.

2. Excerpt: Most contests want only your first X pages or X words, not your whole manuscript, but some want it all. Many need it to be snail-mailed, many don't. Many have specific formatting requirements. Just follow the instructions to the T.

3. Synopsis: A synopsis is generally required and graded. It needs to be compellingly written and match the book in voice and tone. The length will vary, but, again, follow the instructions.

You ain't gonna win if you lose points for not following instructions, even instructions that don't seem logical. FOLLOW THE DANG INSTRUCTIONS. Been there, lost points (and a contest) on that.

Want to see a contest critique sheet? I've included one Authorpreneurship Resources on my website (http://pamelahutchins.com/free-resources/authorpreneurship/) from one of my contest wins to give you a flavor of the elements analyzed and the type of feedback given. This will vary by contest, of course.

Nothing ventured, nothing gained, so venture forth, my friends, and contest, contest, contest.

30 • BE A SOCIAL BUTTERFLY

The optimal use of social media for an author

Love it or hate it, social media is a critical part of marketing. It is a way of connecting, not only with potential readers, but also with people who can help you meet your goals—as long as you remember that it's a two-way street. You need to be prepared to put as much or more energy (or money) into other people's goals as you would like them to put towards yours.

Why is this important? Recap alert: You sell your book by getting people to tell *other* people to buy it, not by screaming "buy my book" over and over on Facebook.

Think of social media as a way to fill a bucket that has the potential to contain goodwill. You will need that goodwill to sell your book. You have to fill your bucket *first*, and you do that by helping others.

The good news is that it is really not very hard to fill your bucket. People are grateful to accept help. If you get out and establish an online presence and help people promote whatever it is they are trying to sell/distribute/raise for charity, they will be a hundred times more likely to do the same for you when the time comes.

The bad news is, the bucket has a leak. If you fill it up and then get busy doing other things for a few months, you will come back and find that the bucket drained dry while you were away. This is why everyone says that social media is hard. It's not hard to get the bucket full, but it is hard to *keep it that way* while you are trying to do all the other things you have to do.

The other critical reason to be active in social media? To give people an easy way to learn about you and your books, to discover that they like you and care about what you have to say. Think about that every time you use Facebook, Goodreads, Google+, Twitter, Instagram, or Pinterest. The people you meet in your social networks know you only by the snippets you give them, and they will likely only see a fraction of what you post. Make sure you show them the version of you that you want people to see. Be interesting, be funny, be smart, be scientific, be creepy, be yourself—with lots of colors. But be careful; don't be reckless. If you write Christian-themed children's stories, you probably don't want to go off on an expletive-filled rant about how you want to kill everyone at your local grocery store, even if they are a bunch of morons.

Social media is public and permanent

A few words of caution: do not fool yourself into thinking you have any privacy online. You better be sure you want to put it out there, all the way out there, before you hit Enter. If you are taking cracks at your spouse on Facebook or if you want to post those great pictures of yourself doing tequila body shots during your Mexico vacation, just know that you will NEVER be able to pull them back, no matter what your privacy settings are. Be mindful of this even when you are leaving comments on blogs. Choose your user name wisely and your words carefully. If someone Googles you, your comments under your real name may all come up.

Also, if you are using social media to actively push a social, political, or religious agenda, this may work for you and fit your goals, but it also may narrow your list of potential readers. And that may be *fine* with you. I just want you to remain realistic. You may write romantic thrillers, which have a broad audience; however, if your social-media presence is over-the-top conservative (like a few of my family members'), you will probably cut your market in half. Do you really not want to sell your book to those crazy liberals, even when they use the same currency you do? People beyond your social network can and will see your posts, especially on Goodreads.

So let's talk about Goodreads.

Goodreads = Virtual heaven for indie authors

If you're an indie author and you're not on Goodreads, it's time to take the plunge. Recently acquired by . . . you guessed it, Amazon, with a rapidly growing community of readers and authors numbering over ten million—thanks to integration with Facebook Timeline—and a data partnership with industry giant Ingram, Goodreads is the leading social-media site for bookophiles. We congregate to swap recommendations and reviews, interact in like-minded groups and clubs, and enter our names to win swag from authors. Goodreads has competitors, like LibraryThing and Shelfari (also owned by Amazon), but they're pale in comparison.

For many overwhelmed, overworked, and underpaid authors, the thought of another social-media site (or any social-media site) may cause tremors. Goodreads makes it easy, though, starting with their Author How-To (http://www.goodreads.com/author/how_to). The How-To has slide shows to guide you step-by-step through creating your author profile and much, much more. In fact, they teach you *how* to do just about everything I'm going to recommend.

Before I start with the tips, though, it's important to understand that I believe these have the greatest likelihood of driving users to engage with you and ultimately read, rate, and review your books, thus driving other users to engage with you in the same way. Every time people add, rate, or review your books, their Goodreads friends see notifications and are influenced to do the same thing. And some of those people actually purchase your books.

So here are the tips:

1. Create a dynamic author profile

Yeah, yeah, you've done this before and it's called a website. I know. But none of the ten-million-plus Goodreads users want to leave Goodreads, which for them is one-stop shopping. In fact, the only time they leave will be to buy your book, so take advantage of all the bells and whistles Goodreads lets you add to your profile, and engage your community on its home turf. Do the expected things well: write interesting copy, post a quality photo, and make sure all your books are linked to your profile.

Tchotchkes to keep users coming time and again? Add your blog feed. To engage them with you directly? People love videos. To show them you're for real? Add your events, like signings, readings, seminars, and releases. You can even browse through your friend list and let specific people know of your events in their area. I've done just about everything Goodreads offers, so feel free to steal ideas from my profile (http://www.goodreads.com/pamelafaganhutchins). You can friend me or fan me while you're there and it won't hurt my feelings a bit.

2. Shelve, rate, and review books

Goodreads is a reader community, so share what you're reading. You can put books on your To-Read shelf, and when you're done, you can rate and even review them. HINT: you can copy and paste the same review onto Amazon (or vice versa) as well. Take the time to rate and review your favorite books, too. Building your ratings lists teaches Goodreads how to recommend books to you, and your biggest fans will love seeing what you think of other literature. You could go even further by creating a shelf of your Influences or Favorites. And although Goodreads lets you rate and review your own books, know that rating is generally OK, but reviewing . . . well, just say no.

3. Add Goodreads widgets to your own website

There are free widgets that let you invite visitors to your website to add, rate, and review your books on Goodreads. Here's an example from my nonfiction book page (http://pamelahutchins.com/publications/nonfiction/). Even better is the widget that streams reviews from Goodreads to your website. Check this example out (http://pamelahutchins.com/, then scroll down to the middle of the page) to see how well this feature can work for you. Also, while you're out there, note the widget in the right-hand column that shows all the books I've rated and reviewed. Sweet! Now Goodreads is influencing visitors to my site who may not even be Goodreads users themselves.

4. Run giveaways

Over 40,000 users per day participate in giveaways on Goodreads. As I mentioned in chapter twenty-eight, giveaways make readers much more likely to notice, add, read, rate, and review your books. The people most likely to do these things are the winners themselves, *so give away as many books as you can*. I gave away twelve copies of *Saving Grace*, and I think that was largely responsible for it being added to over 1,130 To-Read shelves. It generated a number of ratings and reviews, as well. I was able to get more than one hundred ratings before I released the next book in the series.

5. Be active in your communities.

Goodreads has more than 20,000 book clubs, each of them with unique members and rules. Keeping in mind that Goodreads is a reader community, join some groups, familiarize yourself with the rules, and start chatting with other readers about books . . . any books but your books. Over time, as you become a contributing member of a group, you can approach the moderator to ask for a facilitated discussion of one of your books, but please make that transition a natural one, or you'll make all of us look like used-car salesmen. You can even create a discussion group for your own book, complete with videos and polls for optimal user engagement.

Lists work much the same way, and there is a list for every topic imaginable on Goodreads. My recent favorite? Indie Authors Everybody Should Read (http://www.goodreads.com/list/show/25972.Indie_Authors _Everybody_Should_Read?format=html&page=1).

Once you earn a hundred or so ratings and at least a 4-star average, Goodreads starts to include your book in promotions, much like I described earlier with Amazon. Sweet!

The long and the short of it

How does all this translate to book sales? It's really impossible to quantify. But if you look at the Goodreads activity for titles that are selling on Amazon and in bookstores, you'll see that it's quite strong, which suggests correlation, at least, if not causation. Causation comes from you—your actions and your book.

If you were to pick only one social-media site for reader engagement, I'd recommend Goodreads. I believe that you'd be hard-pressed to find a site better focused on your target market. But experiment with Facebook and Twitter, too, and see what works for you. While these are, in my opinion, the top three sites for indie authors, many people find Instagram, Pinterest, and Google+ useful as well. Google+ is becoming more important as it integrates with the Google search engine and increases your visibility the more you use it.

Social networking can be a little overwhelming, given that you have something approximating a real life to live and all. It doesn't have to be a full-time job, though. Services like

Tweetdeck (http://tweetdeck.com) can save time by letting you manage all your social-media sites in one place. Once you get the hang of it, effective social networking should take only half an hour per day, less if you're efficient.

31 • SPEAK UP, THEY CAN'T HEAR YOU

The importance of speaking engagements and how to do them well

Many writers are, by nature, creatures that hide from the spotlight. I'm not above hibernating for weeks on end in my sleepy sheep pajamas. Yet those of us who publish need to spread the word about ourselves and books. Sure, we can use social media, but at some point, if you really want to gain exposure, you'll have to interact with people in person. Even if you hire a publicist, he or she will not be able to get much traction for you unless you're willing to appear and speak in public. Forget media—you need to sell books, speak, and do events to get people's attention. Plus—oops—members of the media are humans, too.

So let's talk about human interaction. Public speaking, in particular. Most successful authors agree that speaking is a heck of a great way to promote and sell books (http://michaelhyatt.com/why-public-speaking-is-so-important-for-authors.html). I sell books at every speaking engagement I book. That's pretty good incentive to do them, yet the mere thought terrifies most people, let alone introverted writers. I can't help you with your fears—try *Talk Up Your Book* (http://www.matilijapress.com/TalkUpYourBook.html) for that—except maybe your fear of what to speak on, to whom, and how to do it.

What is there to talk about, anyway?

Do you write nonfiction?

Pitch a topic related to your book to groups who share an interest. Maybe you write about remodeling old houses. If so, contact historical societies. Google is your friend. (I should have made that the subtitle of this book.) I write on, amongst other things, ADHD and autism-spectrum parenting, so I give a talk called "Everyone Blames The Mother" for special-needs parenting groups.

Do you write fiction?

Parse out a subject or location from your book. Say you write American Revolutionary historical fiction. Pitch it to the Daughters of the American Revolution. I write women's mystery novels set in the Caribbean, so I speak to travel groups about living and traveling in the Caribbean.

Do you have an interesting day job?

I share stories with book clubs and writers' groups about workplace investigations. To find them, I use Google and Goodreads. Who wouldn't want to come to something called "Colonel Mustard In The Conference Room With His Pants Down," after all?

Do you have insights about authorship?

Some of you are qualified to speak on writing and indie publishing to writers' groups or meetings. I have writer friends that teach agent pitches, synopsis writing, creative writing, the writing practice, and many other topics. I do one called "Deliberate Creativity." Your local writers' group is a great place to start, but, again, your best friend Google opens all doors.

What's in it for you?

Each time I speak—whether at a private location, a library, or a bookstore—I sell books. How many? Depends on the size of the group, but usually about ten. I take my entire backlist no matter what I'm speaking on or for whom, although sometimes the topic really dictates the bulk of what sells at a particular gig.

How to prepare for a speaking engagement

Whether you're meeting your audience in a bookstore, lecture hall, private home, or online, you'll want to plan what you will talk about. Prepare your speaking notes and any visuals or handouts you will use. Practice giving your speech to a friendly audience, like your dog, and as you improve, move on to a harsher one, like your cat. Graduate to demo'ing for your loved ones until you can get through your presentation without a cold compress and smelling salts.

On location

Secure permission from your contact to bring and sell books and ask for a small table on which to display your wares. Pack a wheeled suitcase with your supplies: books, signing pen, giveaway items like bookmarks and business cards, and paper to record the e-mail addresses of readers who want to stay in touch or hear about your new releases. Be prepared to take cash, check, and charge. I recommend selling your books for a number ending in 0 or 5 for ease of making change. Do you own an iPad or iPhone? Try out Square Register (https://squareup.com/register). It's a cheap and easy way to turn your phone into a cash register that accepts credit-card swipes. If you can, bring a buddy to help with logistics and your first-time nerves.

Online

Is your audience in another town? No problem. In fact, fewer problems. You'll eliminate your wheeled suitcase and cash-register issues, plus the stress of following the spotty directions yielded by your iPhone and the inevitable traffic snafus that pop up when you're most pressed for time and least emotionally equipped to handle them. Use Skype (http://skype.com) to video-connect for free. You won't be able to sell physical books, but you can still gently encourage attendees toward e-commerce or a bookstore.

Want to speak from the comfort of your home but still deliver an interactive experience to your audience? You can buy a one-user license for Adobe Connect (http://www.adobe.com/products/adobeconnect/webinars.html) and host webinars for up to one hundred people at once. Love it!

Personally, I think I've only begun to scratch the surface. Who knows how many books I could sell if I pursue more speaking opportunities? I definitely know how many I'll sell if I sit at home.

32 • BOOK IT, DANNO

Planning and holding book events that sell books, build relationships, garner media, and please booksellers

The thought of signing books at your very own event may be the epitome of author awesomeness for many of you. It is a lovely dream. Lines of people waiting patiently for hours for the honor of watching you scribble their name and yours into a book you wrote.

The reality is that book signings are a hard sell, even for the traditionally published writer. Book *sales* are a hard sell, and at a signing, you're asking people to come buy your books at a specific time in return for your smiling face and John Hancock. Your mama thinks those are special, but to most people, they aren't much of an enticement. If you're indie, you'll have to work hard and smart to hold a dynamite book signing, but you can achieve fantastic results if you include certain factors in your plan.

The elements of a great book signing

1. Location, location, location

Don't go holding some random event in an area where you have no following or name recognition. Who the heck is going to come check out the aforementioned *Secret History of Rhode Island Basket Weavers* unless they already know the book—and even better, you? The only answer: no one. You won't even get a polite drop-by from the janitor unless you went to high school with him. Why? Because people are afraid that even talking to you will result in them having to buy crap they don't want. Right? That's why you scurry past the vendor-person when you see him, too. You know you do.

So pick a location where people know of you or your book. Where you can draw a crowd that came specifically to see you and buy what you are selling. Otherwise you're going to sit by yourself for two hours playing tiddlywinks and pretending you aren't devastated.

Some stores charge you for the signing. You probably won't recoup the cost. Especially if you're footing the bill for grub and giveaways. I don't pay for book signings. I do, however, partner with the store to promote them. So I don't talk about e-books when I'm in the world of brick and mortar. I do suggest to customers who buy my books that they take some time in the store and consider purchasing some of the fine merchandise available above and beyond mine. To me, it's all about making the bookseller feel the event was worthwhile. If they made money, I probably did, too, and they may invite me back or become a reference for me. More on that below.

Don't sit around waiting for stores to invite you. Seek them out, introduce yourself, ask them to carry your books, and request a signing. The words "on consignment" can work wonders in indie stores, since they have to pay the distributor up front for inventory from traditional publishers, and with you, they can sell your books first and pay you back later. If the books don't sell, the distributor may return part of the store's investment when they pulp the remaining books, but *your* books won't cost the store a cent. Consignment is a magical, wonderful word to them.

2. Timing is everything

You want shiny, happy people who don't feel rushed. You don't want them fighting traffic to get to your event. They need time to chitchat with you while you sign the book they buy, and then time to browse the store and buy other products your host has to offer. So pick a day and time that allows for a leisurely pace.

3. And who doesn't love free food?

Bring food if the store will let you. If you offer an alcoholic beverage, be sure to provide a nonalcoholic choice as well as snacks.

4. Hell, who doesn't love free *anything*?

Give your bookmarks or other small promotional items to every person who stops to talk to you. Ask the booksellers if they are running any specials in conjunction with your signing that you can promote for them; this may even provide them with a hint. And, finally, consider making your signing a Q&A or a workshop. Sure, you can still sign and sell books, but the store and you need traffic, so give people something of value *for free* to get them to come in.

5. Secure commitments

Don't take it for granted that your best friend Martha will come and bring her roommate and her roommate's boyfriend's stepmom. Promote your event. Facebook Events is a good way to start getting the word out. I also like Goodreads events, which allows me to identify and invite friends in different areas. I occasionally use Evite (http://evite.com) to send cute invitations to my contacts via e-mail, and then post my Evite on Facebook. I send it to my invitees again through Facebook inbox. By then, they're ready to kill me, but they've found they can't ignore me. I can also use Evite to send reminders to those who RSVP'd yes, and I can tickle those who failed to respond.

I don't stop there. I also ask the store if there is anything they can do to promote the event, like put posters in their lobby or handbills by the cash registers (which I print and mail to them, or e-mail if I trust them to do a decent job of the printing themselves). I ask if they have recommendations for promoting it in the community, like on local bulletin boards or community Facebook pages. If the business has a Facebook page, I link to it in my Facebook Event. I ask them to post the Event on their wall. Finally, I send personal e-mails or I pick up the phone and talk to the people I want to anchor the event. I need guaranteed attendees to make the event meet my goals. See #1: Location.

None of these things cost more money, but they all require elbow grease.

Successful signings fuel sales.

Once, I held a book signing in a Central Texas town of about 20,000 people. Why? Because I have family there.

Now you might think the first people to buy your books when you release them will be family, and you're right about your mom. And that's about it. The rest may remember to buy them later if they see them somewhere, and if they opened your e-mail announcement about your book release in the first place. Hint: 17% is the average open rate of a Mailchimp e-mail, so they probably didn't open it.

So I held the signing in conjunction with a family event in this town, and then my family orchestrated group visits every fifteen minutes. I sold fifty books in two hours. Because of the buzz my family created, I sold books to people I didn't know, which was cool; one of them even pre-ordered my next book.

My fifty-book sale set a store record for the highest sales by an author at a book signing in their history. With only fifty. Does that tell you something, people? Unless you're Kim Kardashian, you just don't sell in volume at signings. Heck, I was elated with fifty. It blew my expectations out of the water, and the store manager said he would have considered ten a very successful signing. But what else did I get out of it? Why was it soooo worth my time?

I sold books. Have you noticed yet that it is hard to sell books? It is. And each book is more than a book, it is also like a business card. I may have sold them primarily to family, but those were fifty books that they wouldn't have purchased or read otherwise, and that may have inspired them to buy more as gifts, tell others about them, or pass them along to others who might read them, buy more, talk about them, and pass them on. Grassroots, people.

I ingratiated myself with the store, which sold a lot more than my books to my customers. They did a thousand dollars in business related to my signing. The manager was bouncing up and down on his toes when he showed me the numbers.

As a result of my "popularity," the store moved all my books to an endcap with a "Signed Copies Available" display. That placement alone sells books and makes me look IM-POR-TANT. Before, they'd stuffed me in a corner under Humor. You could only find me if you asked at the front counter.

Which brings up a truth: just being stocked in a store is not enough. You need placement. Which my husband and children and editor occasionally provide for me when they browse a bookstore and see my books shelved in a less-than-ideal location. Woopsie, should I have just typed that??

The store gave me a reference to its corporate office and other locations. I booked more signings elsewhere as a result. And, ultimately, this corporation carried my books chain-wide. Hastings Entertainment, have I told you lately that I love you?

Events give me material for blog posts and social-media promotion. I need that material, because *I don't tell people to buy my books* on Facebook or Twitter. I tell them when I am on a radio show, or when I have a signing, or when an article about me appears in the local paper. So even if my signing is a flop, I have something to promote that links to my books, and none of my online community has to know I ate all the fruit and cheese myself, right?

I have one last tip for you. It's about volume. I have a large number of published books. I make sure multiple copies of them are available at every event. Many customers buy three or more titles. I would never have sold fifty books that day if I wasn't a multi-title author. It's worth thinking about. If you hold off publishing your first book until you get that second or third book ready, you will have a lot more vroom vroom in your sales engine, whether readers find you at a signing, online, or in a bookstore.

Bottom line: success starts with goal-setting and realistic expectations. You can do successful book signings as an indie author, but not without careful planning and a great deal of the *right* effort. Don't overbook yourself with poorly timed or poorly executed signings. Pick the right location within the right community, get firm commitments from anchor attendees, and give more than you get, in terms of your expertise, your snacks (!), and your promotion.

33 • BECOME A MEDIA DARLING

How to get and give good media

Once upon a time in another life, I had a real job. Not that I don't work now, but it's pretty hard to convince people I have a real job when most days I sport pj's until I hear the dogs barking at the side door, alerting me to my husband's return from *his* real job and leaving me mere seconds to transform from my happy-but-haggish self to almost-put-together office-at-homer. In that old life, I was the vice president of Human Resources and Legal for a refining company in the Caribbean. I wore Ellen Tracy suits, Puerto-Rico-high heels, and (sometimes) makeup. I dispensed justice from my large office. People said "Yes, ma'am" to me and gave me stock options.

Unfortunately, I hated it. I liked some of the people I worked with a lot. In fact, one of them I liked so much that I ditched my job and married him. (Yes, Eric.) But even though I am so much happier in my new life, I experienced some amazing things in that old job.

One of those amazing things? Media training. That's right. Media, as in TV, radio, and print. The awesome T.J. Walker of Media Training Worldwide (http://mediatrainingworldwide.com/) came from New York to our little island to teach some of us how to talk to reporters. I was the communications officer of the Incident Command Staff, which meant that in the event of a crisis, I could end up in front of a camera, talking to a slick reporter. Yikes.

All of this wisdom comes in handy now when I appear publicly or give interviews about the books I've written. That only happens, though, when I pursue it. No journalists are beating a path to my door. I doubt they will for you, either. As an indie writer, you've accomplished something huge and wonderful, but you are invisible to the world unless you get out there and introduce yourself. This means that you submit story pitches woven into press releases—that would, by golly, make perfect stand-alone articles—to newspaper, magazine, radio, and TV people. And then you do it again. You make it so easy and relevant to their readers, viewers, and listeners that they'd be crazy not to use the copy you put together for them.

Planning for interviews

T.J. put us through grueling workshops where we crafted our message points for pretend disasters and delivered them in videotaped statements. He grilled us with questions and critiqued our responses. He forced us to write and stick to our water-cooler message points, the three things we wanted people talking about at work the next day.

"No matter what they ask you, circle back to an answer that cites at least one of your three water-cooler messages, and preferably all three," T.J. advised. "Tell stories. Even though you wouldn't do this in writing, use clichés that people can latch onto. If it's live, vary your tone, keep your upper body still, and use hand gestures and facial expressions that match your words. Keep your answers in short sound bites, nothing longer than thirty seconds. Remember who your audience is, and talk directly to their interests."

The first time I scored a TV appearance about my books, I wrote down the three water-cooler points I wanted to get across. I listed questions I was likely to be asked, then prepared answers that referred to my points. The news show would run only two minutes of footage, so I needed any single answer to communicate what I wanted people to take away about me and my books. What I did *not* want to do was appear to be making a sales pitch. I wanted to provide a taste of what they—and I—were about.

The hardest part? Picking out what I'd wear and coiffing camera-ready hair. The best part, besides hitting all my message points, was that it was fun. Nerve-racking, yes, but really, really fun.

Expect the unexpected

While TV is fun, radio is the bomb. I lo-o-o-o-o-v-e doing radio. Especially when I'm the call-in guest. Call-in guest = Pamela doesn't have to change out of her pj's or do her hair to talk to thousands of people over the airwaves. Mishaps, however, can arise, and planning is still crucial.

Case in point: one day I had put on my very best pair of sleepy sheep pj's and my telephone headset and was sitting by the phone at the appointed time for a call from a radio station. The phone rang. I said hello.

"Stand by to join Dr. Hotze after the commercial break," a woman said.

"I'm ready," I replied.

The music came on, signaling the start of the show. Dr. Hotze and his co-host, Brooke, talked for a while, then it was my turn to speak.

As I opened my mouth, my next-door neighbor's lawn crew fired up their industrial mower.

VROOM VROOM VROOM VROOM VROOM VROOM VROOOOOOOOOOOOM!

I was in a panic. I did my best to answer their questions during the first segment, then we broke to commercial. Oh, spit!! I was tied to the phone, tethered by its cord, unsure how long I had until the interview resumed. I cast about for solutions for the awful background noise, but about all I accomplished was to fret myself into a nervous sweat. But then the mower moved to the other side of the yard. It was better. It was good enough.

The cue music started. Dr. Hotze asked me a question.

VROOM VROOM VROOM VROOM VROOM VROOM VROOOOOOOOOOOOM!

T.J. Walker didn't teach me how to handle the noise of industrial mowers, and I was on a hard-wired landline with a short cord, so I couldn't run away from the sound. Eric had replaced our cordless phones with this old-timey model because he could never get the kids to put the phones back on their chargers. It had seemed like such a brilliant move at the time. Not so much now. I stalked to the farthest point I could stretch the cord to as the lawnmower roared in the background.

The segment ended. We went to commercial. By now, sweat was dripping down my sides and pooling in my bra. Flannel pj's were no longer the ideal outfit, and this was not how I had pictured this interview going down.

When the mower headed toward the back yard, I thanked God. I could do the last segment in peace.

The music cued the start of the last segment and I cleared my throat, ready to begin.

VROOM VROOM VROOM VROOM VROOM VROOM VROOOOOOOOOOOOM!

This time, the lawn guy was mowing the strip of grass right by my office window. Basically, he had all but lodged himself into the phone's mouthpiece. I had to do something, so I threw myself underneath my desk so the wood could provide an extra barrier between me and the awful noise. It was a little better.

I was pretty sure Dr. Hotze had just asked me, "And so why did you write *Hot Flashes and Half Ironmans*, Pamela?," so I cupped my hand around the mouthpiece and prayed I didn't sound like a heavy-breathing prank caller. I began to think about the fun I would have writing about the experience. I imagined myself away to my happy place, the Annaly tidal pools back on St. Croix, and I hit my message points on autopilot. As soon as the interview was over, the roaring stopped. It had taken them exactly as long as my radio appearance to mow my neighbor's yard.

I'm a damn fine Girl Scout, but that time I had not been prepared. For a Petey-the-one-eyed-Boston-terrier barking emergency? Yes. I had stashed him in the game room with special treats. For call waiting? Uh huh, I'd turned that off. I'd warned the kids, turned off my cell phone, and put a note on the door so no one would call or ring the bell to interrupt us. But I hadn't planned for industrial mowers.

Moral of the story for radio and print interviews from home: plan for the worst. And remember, if nothing else, it will give you something to blog about later.

34 • DON'T FORGET THE LITTLE PEOPLE

Covering a few more critically important promotion topics

You may think that since I've devoted whole chapters to the promotional topics I've covered so far, anything thrown into a multi-topic chapter is only as worthy as the ink spilled for it. Au contraire. This chapter contains some of the most important tips of all, so focus like a laser here.

On publicists

A publicist is a goddess who navigates the world of events and media with ease. She has a contact list that'll make you weep, and she isn't afraid to use it. She loves to dial and smile, and will call anyone (repeatedly) on your behalf. She has form letters and lists of bookstores out the wazoo. Obviously, she can help you. But is she worth the expense? Most publicists charge by the hour; expect to pay $35 to $150 an hour.

Caution: only hire one who will read your book and still want to promote you afterwards. They have to believe in you to be convincing.

I hired a wonderful publicist for *Saving Grace*, and she was invaluable. You are welcome to poach her, if you'd like: Paula Margulies (http://paulamargulies.com). You do not want to know what I'd spent with her by the time I was through the promotion, because even with great lists, forms, and contacts, making calls and writing letters takes time. I would hire her again, but I caution you to be realistic about the cost. If you want to hear it as I told it to her when she interviewed me for an online article, check out the appendix and catch us chatting there.

Paula did three main things for me: wrote and distributed press releases, contacted bookstores about potential book events, and contacted media to ask them for coverage.

With chain bookstores, she was initially hamstrung, because my indie-published books were not on their national buy lists—and this was even after we'd made sure they were fully returnable from Ingram. This is likely to happen to you as well, especially if your books are not returnable or are only available on consignment.

With indie bookstores, she was not nearly as successful as my husband at convincing them to carry my books and let me do events—but nothing beats Eric's passion for projects involving me, and vice versa.

Paula did a great job getting me media coverage, including radio, TV, and print (you can see for yourself at http://pamelahutchins.com/about/media/, if you'd like). She also helped me identify contests.

Hiring Paula impressed Barnes and Noble and Hastings Entertainment. Impressing Barnes and Noble got me regional distribution and opened the door to more than fifty book events in one year in their stores.

What my publicist taught me

There's nothing Paula did that you and I could not do ourselves—if we have the time, courage, and determination to develop the forms, lists, and relationships. Those are big ifs. As I said, I'd hire her again. Here are a few of the things we learned:

- How to write a good press release. See the appendix for an example.

- Where to post press releases for free. Two good sites are http://www.prlog.org and http://www.briefingwire.com.

- How to pitch and land book events.

- How to pitch and land media ideas.

- The importance of a list of speaking topics. See an example of mine on my website.

- That her success was 100% dependent on the quality of my book and its cover and editing, my willingness to work hard, my bio, and my ability to fund her endeavors.

Should you hire one?

If you expect a publicist to land you on the *New York Times* best-seller list as an indie author, you may need to adjust your expectations. If you want to increase the visibility of your book and yourself, a publicist can be a great resource. Visibility can lead to sales, agents, and distribution, but it's not a sure thing. Go in with your eyes wide open, and you'll have a good experience.

Here's a resource for finding publicists: The Book Publicity Blog (http://yodiwan.com/2009/02/18/list-of-freelance-book-publicists/).

On advertising

Like publicists, advertising is shiny and tempting. "Maybe if I just spend this money, I'll be a success," many authors think, but they usually find there is no Easy Street to book sales.

Advertising is costly, and the bigger the market the media reaches, the bigger the price tag. We're talking $500 and up in most cases for small print ads in metropolitan newspapers or magazines. Community papers and online ads can be cheaper.

Advertising books vs. events

In general, advertising your book is not very effective. Most readers are not driven to purchase by seeing your ad one time. Most advertising gurus will tell you that a campaign to raise awareness and visibility will be more successful. It will also be more expensive.

However, advertising an event, especially an event at which you will give away books or offer free food and drink, can work fairly well. Media coverage works better for events than for books. We occasionally advertise events, but it's usually to achieve another end. If we're courting a bookseller, our ad for an event in their store gives them free promotion. If we're trying to land an interview with a media station or publication, an ad indicates our enthusiasm and sweetens the pot. While the company line is that advertising sales and media coverage are not linked, we've seen a stunning correlation between interviews booked and ads placed. Just sayin'.

But if I had my choice between advertising and a good publicist, I'd choose the publicist.

On author pages

Don't neglect the opportunity to publicize yourself through Goodreads' (http://www.goodreads.com/author/program) and Amazon's Author Pages (http://amazon.com/author/). These pages may duplicate the bio you lovingly created for your own website, but that's all right. You want to make information about yourself and your books easy to find, so provide it in any medium that allows it.

On little-known sales venues

As you look for ways to increase visibility and sales, consider some creative venues if you have print copies of your books.

Regional book fairs

Not all are indie-friendly, but if they are, this is the place to rub shoulders with librarians and booksellers.

Street festivals, church bazaars, and artisan fairs

Often you'll have to pay a table or booth fee, but these events can be a wonderful way to gain and connect with readers. As long as you don't try to peddle erotica at a church bazaar.

Specialty stores

If there are specialty stores that relate to the topic of your book, consider approaching them to sell your book, too. My *Hot Flashes and Half Ironmans* does well in running, triathlon, bicycle, and swim shops, for instance.

Grocery chains

In my neck of the woods, Kroger has an author program administered by one intrepid writer who screens books and writers into it. If you are accepted, you can set up a table in Kroger grocery stores on weekends and sell books. This works especially well if you are by the deli and coffee shop, and if you do two or three days in a row. Then poor schmucks like me who end up running in to grab something they forgot every day or two will see you more than once.

On book trailers

My digital artist, Heidi Dorey, doubles as a video editor, so we used her for our second book trailer. The cost ranges from a few hundred and up. CreateSpace offers options of trailers for $1,000 and $2,000+. You have to sell a heck of a lot of books to cover that kind of cost. We had a very particular need for a book trailer; had we not, I would not have invested in one. When done well, they make great marketing pieces, and you can upload them to YouTube and embed them on websites wherever you want.

A trailer shouldn't be much more than a minute long—because we are a world of short attention spans—and should show your name, title, and cover long enough to brand them into people's minds. You don't need to tell the story so much as set the tone and evoke an emotional response that leaves people wanting more.

On e-newsletters

I saved the best for last, and its placement rewards the thorough reader:

He who has the largest e-mail distribution list wins.

The end.

OK, not the end. Why does this matter? Because you want a captive audience to whom you can announce new releases and major events. Only a tiny fraction of them will buy your book based on your e-mail. But the first step in visibility, branding, referrals, and ultimate sales is to communicate with the people you know.

Now, there are laws against spamming, so your list must include only people you know or who opted in and who wish to be on it. My advice is to administer your list and e-newsletter cheaply through a service like Constant Contact (http://constantcontact.com) or Mailchimp (http://mailchimp.com). I use Mailchimp, and for any list of less than 2,000 contacts, there's no charge to administer my e-mails, signups, and e-mailing campaigns.

Mailchimp generates HTML code for my website that lets my visitors sign up for my newsletter. Check it out on my home page: http://pamelahutchins.com. (Go ahead and sign up while you're out there; it won't hurt a bit.) Note that I assure registrants of the following: "Sign up to hear about my new releases. I won't share your e-mail with anyone else, and I'll only contact you when a new book comes out." Then I stick to that promise. My list gets two e-mails per year from me.

I find it very easy to create a newsletter by inserting my information, text, and images into one of Mailchimp's templates. I can schedule delivery ahead of time. By the way, Mondays and Fridays stink for e-newsletters, in my experience. Mornings seem best. Mailchimp handles the unsubscribes and "bounces" and removes them permanently. This is a very, very nice feature.

Now, buck up for a dose of truth, friends: most people don't open your e-mail. It's not critical, and they have lots in their inboxes. Expect an open rate of about 30% unless your subject line guarantees them a trip to Tahiti. That's OK; you don't need them all to open it. And even 25% of 2,000 is still 500 souls, who may even forward it or tell others about it. Mailchimp also helps you post the newsletter to social media so even more people see it.

PART SIX:
HOW TO CRASH THE PARTY.

35 • GET IN LINE

How can an indie author get nationwide distribution in chain bookstores?

Most chain bookstores don't want to deal with indies. Some won't even stock books by traditionally published debut novelists. To get your book on chain shelves, you'll have to show them you understand how a store makes money, and that you and your books can make money for them. Honestly, they could care less whether your book is any good or how hard you worked or whether your mommy is really proud of you.

Bookstores care about profits. And they will not order from CreateSpace; they strongly prefer that you print and warehouse your books rather than print them on demand, and they'll make it hard for you if you don't. They only order if you allow returns and if your discount through Lightning Source is sufficient. For some chains, 50% is good enough. For others, 55% or 60% is what it takes to get onto their Maybe list. Remember, they aren't actually getting a discount that large, because the distributor, usually Ingram, takes a cut.

How can you show a chain bookstore that you will positively impact their profitability? Well, it won't involve profits for you in the short run, let me assure you. You'll have to invest your time and money in a way that drives customers—preferably *paying* customers, and even better, *new* paying customers—into their stores.

Maybe the real question is whether this exercise is worth your time and money. But let me explore the issues for you, so you can decide for yourself, since "Pamela, how can I get my book into Barnes and Noble?" is a question I am asked incessantly. The best way I know how to do this is by holding successful events at their stores.

Make sure the store profits

Events, even consignment events, are not no-brainers for stores. They may balk at your proposal, and they have good reason to. The quality of the book and the author reflect upon the store. The event causes work for the staff. The authors themselves sometimes cause issues for the staff. I hear many stories about diva behavior from unknown authors who expect stores to spend money and make sales on their behalf. Folks, that is simply not the store's job. The store is there to operate in a way that makes it most profitable. Experience has taught them that efforts spent to promote book events are not usually profitable unless the author is an A-list celebrity.

If there is any media and promotion of your event, the store expects you to do it, and do it in a way that promotes the event *and the store*, not just you and your book. (Seek permission to use their name and logo for any ads you wish to run.) However, this will not usually result in an event where you the author make more money than you spend.

Why hold a cash-negative event? You should only do it if it either a) makes you happy or b) fits your long-term strategy of up-front investment in your writing career to achieve a long-run goal of ... whatever your goals are. Hint: Having bookstores direct order and stock your books is probably the goal that makes the most sense if you are spending money on event promotion and advertising.

And it can work. I held a consignment event in a Hastings Entertainment store and, with the help of my husband, stacked it for success. We chose a location and a time that gave us a chance to hit the ball over the fence. We advertised and made the store aware of it. We promoted through every possible free channel as well, and made the store aware of that, too. And I sold fifty-five books. This made the store happy. They suggested we call their corporate offices.

We were not profitable on this event.

We called their corporate offices and arranged another event. We sold nearly forty books, and we took all the same steps. The store and the corporate offices were very happy.

We were not profitable on this event.

We asked how we could get the chain to carry my debut novel. They said they didn't do debut novelists, much less indie debut novelists. We said that we understood and asked again. They said, "We'll stock you in five stores regionally. You sell those stores out, and we'll talk."

We pulled out all the stops to drive traffic to those stores.

We were not profitable in those actions.

We sold the stores out. The chain stocked more stores. We sold them out. We booked a series of events that were not profitable for us, but were great for the stores. We averaged selling twenty-five books per event.

THE STORE ORDERED MY FIRST NOVEL CHAINWIDE.

Two months later they informed us they had deemed the title "performing" and were reordering in some locations. They told us that the residual sales in stores and cities where we held events were strong. They ordered another of my books chainwide.

We started to inch toward profitability, although we weren't there yet.

What had we done? We had invested in a business that we believed in—a start-up small press—and set a goal of turning a profit by the fourth novel.

Did you just throw up a little in your mouth? Because I'd understand if you did. But think about it for a second. What do you think the small presses and major houses do? They invest in authors as brands and get them out to the masses, then drop them if they're not taking off after the second or third book.

If you want to get distribution in chain stores, you'll have to act like a publisher, not like an author. A good number of you won't care to do this. That's OK. It's a lot of work and expense, and there's no guarantee of a return on your investment.

After our "success" with Hastings Entertainment, we turned our attention to Barnes and Noble. Barnes and Noble has a Small Press Department, which evaluates books from small and indie presses and passes some of those along to their book buyers for consideration. Barnes and Noble has only one fiction buyer, nationally, or so we are told by our contacts in the Small Press Department. That buyer picked up my first novel regionally. This was important not just because it landed my book in some stores, but also because it got *Saving Grace* into Barnes and Noble's ordering system, and the stores are only allowed to order books that make it into this system.

Important rabbit hole: Back when we did my books through CreateSpace, the Barnes and Noble stores did not order them. Even when we did them through Lightning Source, the Barnes and Noble stores didn't want anything to do with them unless they were in the Barnes and Noble system, even though they were in the Ingram system. Heck, even after we were in their system and distributed regionally, some Barnes and Nobles refused to order *Saving Grace* for customers because they insisted that they do not do "print on demand." I'll get back to this point in a moment.

Repeat alert: How did we get the national fiction buyer to add *Saving Grace* to the Barnes and Noble system and warehouse and stock *Saving Grace* regionally? We submitted per their website's instructions. And our submission was the mother of all indie marketing plans. You can view our cover letter to the Barnes and Noble Small Press Department (https://www.box.com/s/c57j7vvsvw6mhfhckezn) and our marketing plan for *Saving Grace* as presented to Barnes and Noble Small Press Department (https://www.box.com/s/4j3q4zmrojtjwyywykk9) online and in the appendix to *Loser*.

Once we'd developed a relationship with the Small Press Department, we requested consideration for expansion of our region. They gave us some nifty tips. First, hold events. Well, we already knew that, right? They said that store managers can order books even if they're not stocked in their stores, and if a title sells well at an event, the manager may choose to continue to stock it. If it doesn't sell well, the books will be returned.

Interestingly, we found that even if a title sells quite well, some managers return the extras no matter what. It's less about sales and more about a particular manager's philosophy about what to stock. We find Barnes and Noble very prone to returns, which is unfortunate, because it deprives the store of the residual impact of buyers we reached through local promotion and advertising, and it costs us a pretty penny on returns. We think it's short-sighted. But we don't run the stores.

Think global, buy local (even from chains)

The second tip from the Small Press Department was to encourage people to order books from brick-and-mortar Barnes and Noble stores. We did this, and the hassle factor was high, but the long-term impact was very positive.

The hassle? Some store employees balked on ordering as soon as they saw "print on demand." Barnes and Noble does not have a corporate policy against purchasing print on demand. They do, however, require returnability. Many employees, even managers, don't understand the difference. We barely understood it at first. Our friends out shopping at our behest didn't understand it. One by one we helped the stores understand it, and that the returnability they needed was promised on the next screen. Once the stores broke down to order one book, we found they often ordered two to five. If those sold within a certain time period, they ordered—wait for it—TWENTY-FOUR. Wow. We were on to something.

Our chain strategy

And this was when we decided to spend money with Barnes and Noble just when we'd broken even on our chain venture with Hastings Entertainment.

"Hey," our thinking went, "let's cluster a bunch of geographically dispersed events close together and load them for success."

We wanted to show Barnes and Noble's national fiction buyer a pattern of quick sales after store orders, and a volume of sales in a short time period. We wanted to hold events at stores and get my books into them, to build relationships with store staff, to aim for nationwide distribution, and to increase visibility and readership. Good bookseller relationships could pave the way for books by other authors that we will publish through our budding small press in the future.

So we decided to send me out in an RV plastered with my book decals and web address to do a nationwide book tour. We went all out and spent a year building up to this 2.5-month initiative. We identified my potential contacts: alumni groups, book clubs, writers' groups, libraries, and many more. We got in touch with all of them and arranged speaking engagements, media, reviews, postings, and appearances in conjunction with many of the sixty bookstore events we held.

While we initially found it quite difficult to get into some locations, and while we knew we would vastly outspend our profitability on this venture, we also exceeded our wildest expectations for visibility, store orders, and bookseller relationships. At our smallest event, I sold twelve books, but my sixty-store average was twenty-five books per event. In markets I had never entered, like Savannah where I knew not a soul and ran fifty sales through the Barnes and Noble register, I *averaged* twenty-five books. Bookseller after bookseller told us that most authors sold one to five books and that ten was a great day. They loved us. They asked us to teach classes to big publishers. They invited us back. We were thrilled. And, as planned, we didn't make a penny.

What did this venture cost? To begin with, 15,000 miles of gas at $3.75 a gallon and 2.5 months of RV usage, added to an average of $38 per night in RV campground fees. My time. My husband's time. Promotional materials (posters, handbills, and bookmarks) came to $1000. We lived within an advertising budget of $15,000. We spent $10,000 on giveaways. We invested $15,000 in publicity. It was expensive, even on the cheap. Absolutely no volume of conceivable book sales in the same twelve-month period as the book tour could cover the cost.

So why did we do it? As a business investment, with start-up capital to establish a small press. Obviously, that presupposed that we could fund it. We had the money to invest; we know that many people don't.

Would I have done this as a maverick author, a true soloist? Never. Never never never never never.

Would I recommend other maverick authors pursue chains? Not past the initial submission of a marketing plan and holding local events.

Are we pleased that we did the book tour, given our goals for SkipJack Publishing, our expenses, and the results? You betcha. It was a home run. We developed good relationships with booksellers, got fantastic visibility, and connected with new readers.

Chains aren't for everyone.

"But I'm not a small press. I'm just me!" most of you are thinking.

True. Very true. But you guys are the ones asking me at all my events how I got into chains and how you can, too. So there's the whole story. I don't have an answer you want to hear, I fear.

For most indie authors, the pursuit of chain distribution won't be worth the time and money, and I would never recommend it. It was worth it to us, though, because we believe placement in stores provides visibility and drives sales everywhere, and because we'll want to place books by other SkipJack authors before too long.

Bookstores aren't going away anytime soon, despite the dire predictions, because many of them have evolved into entertainment stores that meet a variety of customer needs. And although print sales are dwindling, they won't go away completely, either. It's still an avenue Eric and I believe in enough to invest in. Only time will tell if we were right. If not, well, now you know how much of our retirement fund we squandered chasing this goal.

My final word of advice on chains? Focus on what drives you toward your goals. Skip chains if they don't meet your needs.

36 • WORK IT REAL GOOD

Multipurpose your writing for maximum visibility and monetization.

Once you've written something fabulous, why not multipurpose little slices of it into all kinds of gooey goodness? Submit adapted chapters to magazines as short stories. Post a deleted scene as an outtake on your blog. Buff your character studies and share them as reader extras on your website. I've spun some of my book topics and characters into speaking and teaching topics.

Go beyond promotion and visibility; *sell* some of these slices. Spin a deleted chapter into a novella. Novellas (short novels with 20,000 to 50,000 words) regularly sell for 99¢ on Amazon, and serial novellas are getting hot. I recently watched a hybrid novelist indie publish serial novellas, then turn around and sell the entire series as a set. Methinks she is aiming to entice TV producers.

And don't forget the all-important and completely cheap conversion to audiobook when you have the time and energy.

Be creative. You can monetize more than you think.

37 • BEWARE THE PARTY FOUL

A cautionary tale about gifting Kindle e-books

Just when you think you have the system figured out, something comes along that makes you realize that you *really* don't.

Amazon has this nifty feature related to Kindle e-book purchases. There is a yellow button over on the right-hand side of your book's Amazon screen that allows you to "Give as a Gift."

As an indie author or indie publisher, gifting a book to a potential reader can be a pretty good choice. There are other ways to give your book to someone, and we could get into a lengthy debate about whether it's better to use free Smashwords coupons, send people PDFs, and so on and so forth. There are arguments for each. But this chapter isn't about that choice. It's about what happens when you choose Amazon for e-book gifting.

The "advantage" of gifting a Kindle e-book to a reader is that it should show up as a sale, thereby improving your Amazon sales statistics. Your book's relative sales statistics are so very important in driving future sales that it may be worth it to you to spend money on your own book. Think of it as a form of advertising. Bear in mind that, assuming your prices allow you a 70% royalty (taxes and data-transfer fees aside), you are only actually paying 30% of the sales price of your book, and you'll get the rest back in royalties. Thus, the cost of your advertising is 30% of the cost of your book. However, there is a catch. A BIG catch.

When you buy your own book and gift it to someone, Amazon charges your credit card the full sales price and e-mails the link to the recipient. So, let's say that Pamela Fagan Hutchins buys *Saving Grace* and gifts it to her grandmother. Unless Grandmother Fagan actually downloads the book, *it does not count as a sale for royalty purposes*. In other words, if Pamela's grandmother can't figure out how to download the e-book to her new, never-used Kindle that was lovingly given to her by her doting great-grandchildren (a likely scenario), it does not add to Pamela's number of e-books sold. And, most importantly, Pamela doesn't get paid!

Seriously, *you*, the author, don't get paid. Amazon, for the sale of your e-book, does.

Let me take a moment to let that sink in for you. AMAZON **collects** for the sale of your book, BUT IT DOESN'T **PAY** YOU! Even though that gifting cannot be used on any other item on Amazon. *Really.*

So let's put it in another context. Let's say a friend of yours buys your book as a gift for someone else. But that gifting e-mail gets forgotten, ignored or deleted. Again, a likely scenario. Your friend's credit card gets charged. Amazon gets paid for the purchase of your book. You, the author, get nothing.

Moral of the story: Do everything you can to ensure that the Kindle e-books you purchase (or others purchase) for others are sent to people who actually download them. Only when they are actually downloaded from the link does Amazon count them as a royalty-worthy sale.

Tsk, tsk, Amazon. Not very nice.

38 • RECOVER WITH STYLE

It's not whether you'll make mistakes, but how you'll handle them.

Traditionally, an author has six months to prove sellability before her books are yanked from the shelves. She has longer online, but the most profitable sales to the publisher are hardback books in stores, so they want her to prove out in brick and mortar.

You don't have that problem online. Online is forever. Your books remain for sale until you decide otherwise. You have the chance to change your sales strategy over and over until you find something that works. You can even pull them, edit them, and reload them if the problem is a cover, poor editing, or the content itself.

Read the fine print. (I didn't.)

My first novel became a best-seller on Amazon in its first month, when we had it in KDP Select. Then, at the height of its success, Amazon booted it from KDP Select. Why? Because of an aggregator aggravator. I had, pre-KDP Select, used

Smashwords to place my books with Apple and Kobo. When I removed *Saving Grace* from Smashwords, Apple did not pull it down. Amazon removed me from KDP Select because I was in violation of the exclusivity agreement.

My sales tanked on Amazon immediately. And then I started from nothing on the other web-sales channels. I lost thousands of dollars in this misstep. But I regrouped and restrategized, because online is forever, and you never know when success will strike.

And boom, six months later I lowered the price and drove around the country in an RV with giant pictures of the book on it to visit sixty stores in sixty days, and sales shot back up again. I don't advise this drastic measure. Run an ad on World Literary Cafe instead.

So be brave of heart, and don't let bad sales get you down. Pick your book up, dust it off, and try again. Give each strategy at least six months before you abandon it, though. It takes time for your efforts to bear fruit.

39 • DREAM BIG

Breaking into television and movies

Most of us writer types not only dream of seeing our books in print, but also seeing their names in lights. TV lights. Movie lights. Spin-off-product billboard lights. We dream of the actors who will play our main characters, and we can spend hours casting and recasting the parts. Frankly, Jennifer Aniston is getting a little old to play my Katie, but dang, she's perfect.

In fact, we know that the most successful writers make most of their money in this space. Their numbers are few, but their returns are huge.

Screenplay adaptations

From what I hear from my peeps in the trenches, you'll have as much or more trouble selling your book as a screenplay as you do, well, selling your book. My advice is to focus on book sales and visibility for yourself and your book. Then write another. And another. Make each one better than the last, and more visible. If you do a great job at these things, you'll have something to approach a film agent about.

Film options

Or a production company may approach you with a magic word: OPTION. As in "May I please option your magnificent book for thousands of dollars for a year or two?" An option ties your book up while the production company decides whether to exercise the option, meaning whether they will develop the project. Most optioned books don't go into development. Some books get optioned, then re-optioned, then re-re-optioned. I haven't been this lucky (yet). But bear in mind some good advice from Lisa Grace (author of *Angel in the Shadows* and many others) on J.A. Konrath's blog: Consider smaller production companies that may be likelier to exercise your option, get an entertainment lawyer to negotiate your contract, and negotiate the best option fee up front that you can, but don't rule out back-end monies, in case it does get developed. Don't take it from me, though, go straight to the source (http://jakonrath.blogspot.com/2013/07/guest-post-by-lisa-grace.html).

Haven't gotten a call to option your book yet? Well, it's never a waste to work all your contacts. Stranger things have happened, and it doesn't hurt to dream.

40 • GET STARTED ON YOUR NEXT BIG THING

When I informed my traditionally published friends that I was indie publishing my first five books at one time, they thought I was crazy. Maybe I am. The lead time was certainly lengthy. The work was intense, the learning curve and frustration immense. I had five books to write, consult on, get edited, make covers for, enter into contests, format, publish, and promote. Promote. Promote. Promote. Promote. Promote.

I had a plan, though. My plan was this: I would capitalize immediately on online sales of my backlist to happy buyers while I paved the way for my debut novel.

"But how can you focus on successfully marketing each book to ensure its success? You've got a lot of energy, but you still need time," a friend pointed out.

"You need to slowly milk each book for all it's worth to get any traction," another advised.

A third said, "But there's no crossover between fiction and nonfiction."

I don't disagree with them—for *their* marketing plans. But I had my own plan to develop, for my own books and my own career. If I felt that the first five nonfiction books I published were my whole career, I'd follow the advice I was given. But they're not. They're awesome books, don't get me wrong, and I have sold a lot of them and expect to sell tons more for years to come. They're just not the end-all-be-all focus of my writing. They are the entrée into public (well, semi-public) consciousness for my jewels: my novels. The novels that I am rolling out one by one and promoting in a more "traditional" and focused manner.

And I don't have to worry about the sales projections of a publishing executive who peers down her nose through her half glasses at me as she pronounces my nonfiction too paltry to dabble with. It's not too paltry for ME to dabble with. I don't even need much crossover saleability to make this effort worth it. Hell, I'd written the content for those five books over five years of blogging, anyway, so why let it go to waste? It could do some good for me and for those who bought it. They are very helpful books, after all.

All of this—all of this effort, all of this promotion (radio, print, video, and in-person appearances), all of this nerve-racking exposure—was to build the base of the pyramid that would support my novels. My plan was to learn the business and make my mistakes on those five narrative nonfiction books. For each book I sold, hopefully I gained name recognition and a reader of my future books. With each reviewer I wooed, I built a lasting relationship. With each store that held a signing event, I secured a future signing venue.

And thus by the time I launched my first novel, I had a broader platform to market to and a backlist of titles to sell to new readers. And so on. And so on, for all my future books. That backlist only got better with time as I followed my business plan and editorial calendar and wrote and published additional books, books that are complementary to and appeal to the same audience as my others.

"But Pamela, the average book—traditional or indie published—sells less than one hundred copies per year. Weren't you afraid yours would fail if you did them all at once?" naysayers have asked me.

Here's my dirty little secret: I sold more than that of each of them in the first two months. Lots more. And I know why, too. It's because when someone stops by in person to buy one, they think, ah, heck, why not, and they grab one, two, three, or even four more. And they sometimes come back and buy them as gifts for other people.

This works especially well at book signings. Since I've been published, I've averaged selling twenty-five books per signing, and sometimes have sold more than sixty. The owner of the darling indie River Oaks Bookstore, a woman with nearly forty years in the business, said that twenty books at a signing for a traditionally published and well-promoted author is a really, really good signing in her experience. Hastings Entertainment said the average author at a signing in their stores sells six. My husband used to own an indie bookstore. He said the most he ever saw an author sell was ten, and many authors went away selling zero after sitting for two hours twiddling their thumbs and trying to hide their embarrassment. What makes my signings different?

It isn't that I'm special. It's that I have a lot of books to sell, and that we promote the heck out of my events. Go reread chapter 32 on book events for ideas on how to promote yours.

Are my numbers good because I published five books at once? Well, at least in part. In large part. But it's also because those five print books make it more appealing to bookstores to carry my fiction. The bookstores like working with multi-title authors. Think "economies of scale" in relationships. If I provide five (or six, or seven) books to a store that *sell*, isn't it more worth their time to deal with me than an author with one book that sells, if those sales per book are roughly equal?

I love it when a plan works. I encourage you to set goals and to plan a writing life that moves you toward those goals step by exciting step. If those goals include making money at indie publishing, include an editorial plan for four or more complementary books, and you'll have your best chance at it.

And that brings up a good point to end this book on. This book and the bazillion other books, articles, and online materials out there provide you with information. Lots of it. Some of it is mundane and repetitive. Some of it is groundbreaking and exciting. Some of it is wrong, or simply wrong for you. My goal in sharing my journey with you through *Loser* is not to tell you what you **must** do to succeed. Far from it. For starters, your definition of success is unique to you, as is mine to me.

I can't tell you what you need to do. I can provide you with information, though. It's up to you to decide how or whether to use it. Listen, don't listen. Listen and agree, listen and disagree. That's your part in this process.

My business plan, including my multi-title launch and long-range editorial calendar of complementary books, may not result in me becoming the next Dan Brown. In fact, I know it won't. But I won't be moaning on my deathbed that I never went for the brass ring, full-out leaping from my painted, polished pony with arm outstretched and hand grasping. I'm going for it, y'all, the fun, the excitement, and the potential of indie publishing.

How about you?

APPENDIX: BONUS MATERIALS

MARKETING PLAN AND COVER LETTER

Marketing Plan

Saving Grace

By Pamela Fagan Hutchins

Saving Grace is a women's fiction mystery by bestselling, award-winning Houston, Texas author Pamela Fagan Hutchins. She is also the author of five nonfiction books, and she is a contributing author to four additional books.

Description:

Katie Connell is a high-strung attorney whose sloppy drinking habits and stunted love life collide hilariously in a doomed celebrity case in Dallas. When she flees Texas for the Caribbean, Katie escapes professional humiliation, a broken heart, and a wicked Bloody Mary habit, but she trades one set of problems for another when she begins to investigate the suspicious deaths of her parents on the island of St. Marcos. She's bewitched by the voodoo spirit of an abandoned house in the rainforest and discovers that she's as much a danger to herself as the island's bad guys are. As the worst of her worlds collide, Katie drags herself back to the courthouse to defend her new friend Ava, an island local accused of stabbing the senator she's been sleeping with.

Bio:

Pamela Fagan Hutchins, a former attorney and native Texan, lived in the U.S. Virgin Islands for ten years. She refuses to admit to taking notes for this novel during that time.

Saving Grace is intended primarily for an over-30 female audience.

Marketing for Pamela Fagan Hutchins' *Saving Grace* will be a multi-faceted approach:

I.   National Publicist

SkipJack has engaged Paula Margulies Communications (http://paulamargulies.com). Ms. Margulies is providing:

•   Press releases, such as those attached

•   Speaking engagements (see XII and list of topics attached), at venues such as book stores, libraries, writing conferences, colleges, and universities

•   Signings and readings at bookstores nationwide

•   Obtaining trade reviews (see VIII and attached list)

•   Identifying and entering additional contests appropriate for *Saving Grace*

•   Media (TV, radio, print, online) interviews (see VI)

•   Identifying and promoting *Saving Grace* to book clubs

II.   National Blog Tour

SkipJack has engaged Dorothy Thompson and Pump Up Your Books (http://pumpupyourbooks.com) to provide:

•   Three months of tour stops in which Ms. Hutchins and *Saving Grace* will appear on 45+ blogs geared toward her book. Some of these blogs are syndicated into USA Today, Chicago

Times, Wall Street Journal and other high trafficked publications.

- Kindle Fire HD Promotion which will include a Kindle Fire HD giveaway to bring readers, bloggers and book buyers to the blog stops.

- Personalized Book Trailer which will be especially designed for *Saving Grace*. The book trailer will be featured on YouTube and other media outlet (see IX)

- Special Promotions which will include *Saving Grace* blog tour spotlighted in the sidebar on every page of the Pump Up Your Book site with a specially designed banner which will direct visitors to the tour page. Other promotions include promoting the stops on numerous affiliate blogs, when applicable, as well as full social networking promotions.

- A personalized Blog tour page which will include the *Saving Grace* book cover, book summary, book excerpt, buying information, author photo, author bio including website and blog links, book trailer and tour information, as well as SEO optimization. This personalized tour page will become a permanent site.

- Press Releases for the *Saving Grace* blog tour will be syndicated to press release news sites. The tour will also be advertised through the Pump up Your Book group press releases.

- Pre-buzz for *Saving Grace* tour press release announcement will be posted on a minimum of ten blogs and websites before the tour starts.

- *Saving Grace* will also be included in a Group book trailer which will be publicized by the program for additional exposure.

III. National Distribution/National Visibility

SkipJack Publishing has partnered with Lightning Source to provide a high quality paperback version of *Saving Grace* that is distributed nationally through Ingram, with availability worldwide. SkipJack allows for returns, to help carry some of the book buyers' risk.

• SkipJack has established relationships with book stores throughout the United States to carry *Saving Grace*, and Ms. Hutchins' other books, with the goal being to increase the overall visibility of her books.

• *Saving Grace* has been picked up by Hastings Entertainment for direct purchase through Ingram, and is stocked in their stores. Hastings has been an early focus of SkipJack Publishing because of their strong regional presence and the fact that the home office is in Ms. Hutchins' childhood hometown of Amarillo, Texas.

• Additionally, SkipJack works with indie bookstores nationwide, with books in stores in the U.S. Virgin Islands, Maine, Vermont, Maryland, Minnesota, California, and Texas. Indie bookstores also can access *Saving Grace* through Indie Bound.

IV. Worldwide Free Download Campaign

In order to create a buzz for *Saving Grace*, our initial focus was ebook promotion.

• Through a KDP select campaign on Amazon with simultaneous paid marketing on numerous online sites (World Literary Café, Kindle Book Review, Digital Books Today, and others), the Kindle version of *Saving Grace* was downloaded free over 33,000 times all over the world.

• During the promotional period, *Saving Grace* hit #1 in free downloads on Amazon, as well as in the categories of Women's Fiction and Mysteries/Thrillers (where it is sub-categorized in Womens Sleuths).

• With this step done our focus is now print book sales.

V.   Online and Social Media Community Engagement

Ms. Hutchins has been building her online presence for several years. She regularly engages with her community on issues related to her books. In addition, she is an assertive promoter of others through social media.

•   Her website, http://pamelahutchins.com, has 40,000 hits per year. She writes a weekly blog on this site, which has hundreds of subscribers.

•   Her twitter account, @pameloth, has 3500 followers.

•   Her Facebook page, http://www.facebook.com/pamela.fagan.hutchins.author, has 1300 fans.

•   Ms. Hutchins has a friend list of 500 on Goodreads, http://www.goodreads.com/pamelafaganhutchins, where she is currently running a giveaway and ad for *Saving Grace*

•   Ms. Hutchins publishes a bi-annual newsletter for her new releases to an opt-in list of 2000 people nationwide.

VI. Media

Ms. Hutchins regularly gives interviews about her books. To see her on TV, and hear her on radio and podcast, visit http://pamelahutchins.com/about-2/media/. Publicist Paula Margulies will focus on booking media engagements nationwide to promote *Saving Grace* and events associated with the book.

VII. Print Materials

SkipJack retained graphic designer Heidi Dorey to create custom bookmarks, business cards, fliers, posters, ads, and banners for *Saving Grace*. Ms. Dorey designed the cover for the book as well, and is designing the covers for the other books following *Saving Grace* in the Katie & Annalise series. See attached samples.

VIII. Trade Reviews

• A Kirkus review is underway and will likely be completed by the time this package is received in your offices.

• A review by the Houston Press is underway, at their request.

• Copies of *Saving Grace* have been shipped with request for review to an additional 31 highly-regarded trade reviewers (list attached).

• *Saving Grace* has received 60+ reviews on Amazon in its debut month (4.7 of 5.0 stars), has been rated by 40+ reviewers on Goodreads (4.35 of 5.0 stars), and has been reviewed by a number of book bloggers (4 and 5 star reviews) (sample list attached).

IX. Video Book Trailer and Distribution

A Personalized Video Book Trailer is being created for *Saving Grace*. The book trailer will be featured on YouTube and other media outlets, as well as through Ms. Hutchins' online and social media presence.

X. Awards

Saving Grace has already won several awards (Houston Writers Guild Ghost Story Contest 2012 and Writers League of Texas Manuscript Contest 2010), and we plan to enter it into additional competitions in 2013.

XI. Giveaways

SkipJack has made the following giveaways possible to promote *Saving Grace*:

• Kindle Fire HD Promotion which will include a Kindle Fire HD giveaway to bring readers, bloggers and book buyers to the blog stops on the Pump Up Your Book blog tour.

• 33,000+ Kindle copies on Amazon.

• Numerous paperback copies of *Saving Grace* for a variety of contests, including one currently running on Goodreads.

XII. Speaking Engagements

Ms. Hutchins is a dynamic professional speaker, with a past professional membership in the National Speakers Association. Publicist Paula Margulies is booking speaking engagements for her, nationwide (see attached list of topics). In addition, Ms. Hutchins is a regular speaker on employment practices topics in her capacity as an employment attorney and human resource consultant, on behalf of the successful human resources consulting practice she established in 1996 (http://epspros.com).

XIII. Advertising

SkipJack advertises events, when appropriate, such as book signings, book releases, and giveaways. SkipJack has utilized online and print media for such advertising in the past and plans to continue to do so.

XIV. Publications

Ms. Hutchins is a regular contributor to:

• Print: the newsletters of writing organizations in Texas, such as the Houston Writers Guild Scribbler and the Bay Area Writers League.

• Online: BlogHer (http://BlogHer.com), {a mom's view of ADHD} (http://adhdmomma.com), and SkipJack Publishing's blog (http://SkipJackPublishing.com)

XV. Series: Continued Promotion of *Saving Grace*

Saving Grace is the first book in the Katie & Annalise series. Two other books for this series are already written and edited.

XVI. Additional Events

SkipJack held a book launch party for *Saving Grace* on November 3, 2012 (see attached release party information).

The event was held at the prestigious River Oaks Bookstore in Houston. Ms. Hutchins sold 65 books sold at the event, which was advertised in the Houston Press.

XVII.   Complementary Marketing Campaigns

Ms. Hutchins also works with SkipJack to distribute and market her nonfiction books. At her public events, she regularly sells 50+ nonfiction books. These books, listed on an attachment, are primarily relationship humor. Three have won national and regional awards.

Publicist Paula Margulies is also working with Ms. Hutchins on a nationwide promotion of How to Screw Up Your Kids and its just-released companion book How to Screw Up Your Marriage, a one-two punch on blended families and stepcoupling/second marriages.

Awards: How to Screw Up Your Kids was named the Award-Winner in the 'Parenting/Family: Divorce' category of The 2012 USA Best Book Awards, sponsored by USA Book News. In addition, it won the Narrative Nonfiction Award for 2012 from the Houston Writers Guild. Also in the 2012 USA Best Book Awards, Puppalicious and Beyond won a finalist award in Narrative Nonfiction, and Hot Flashes and Half Ironmans won a finalist award in Women's Health.

Cover Letter

The Small Press Department

Barnes & Noble

122 Fifth Avenue

New York, NY 10011

Dear Sir/Madame:

We are requesting consideration of the enclosed novel, *Saving Grace* by Pamela Fagan Hutchins, for inventory for Barnes & Noble stores. We have enclosed a copy of the book, press releases, marketing plan and supporting materials, as well as this letter, per the website instructions.

Saving Grace is the debut novel by Ms. Hutchins. It is a women's fiction mystery. It won the 2010 Writers League of Texas Manuscript Contest (Romance) and the 2012 Houston Writers Guild Ghost Story Contest.

Katie Connell is a high-strung attorney whose sloppy drinking habits and stunted love life collide hilariously in a doomed celebrity case in Dallas. When she flees Texas for the Caribbean, Katie escapes professional humiliation, a broken heart, and a wicked Bloody Mary habit, but she trades one set of problems for another when she begins to investigate the suspicious deaths of her parents on the island of St. Marcos. She's bewitched by the voodoo spirit of an abandoned house in the rainforest and discovers that she's as much a danger to herself as the island's bad guys are. As the worst of her worlds collide, Katie drags herself back to the courthouse to defend her new friend Ava, an island local accused of stabbing the senator she's been sleeping with. Ms. Hutchins, a former attorney and native Texan, lived in the U.S. Virgin Islands for ten years. She refuses to admit to taking notes for this novel during that time.

Ms. Hutchins is also the winner of the 2012 USA Best Books Award for Parenting/Family: Divorce, and a finalist in 2012 for Women's Health and also for Nonfiction: Narrative, with three different relationship humor books. She won the 2010 and 2011 Contemporary Fiction awards from the Houston Writers Guild, and their 2012 Nonfiction award. She is an attorney and entrepreneur as well as an author. She has five nonfiction books with SkipJack as well as *Saving Grace*. SkipJack will publish her follow-up novel in 2013. It will be titled *Leaving Annalise* and it will be the second of a three-book Katie & Annalise series, the third of which, *Missing Harmony*, is also fully written.

SkipJack Publishing is a small publisher that, at present, publishes only Ms. Hutchins. However, we anticipate publishing other authors as well, starting in 2013.

Sincerely,

Eric Hutchins

HOW TO HELP AN INDIE AUTHOR

I'm sure the indie author in your life would appreciate any efforts you make on her behalf, even if you stop after the first suggestion in this article. But, heck, why not try them all? Any of us can eat a very large elephant, if we just do it one bite at a time (and preferably utilize vacuum sealed freezer bags, because it's going to take you a while). I will not address the vegan/vegetarian ramifications of this last statement; suffice it to say that I truly meant "can" and not "will want to." Now, back to the topic of promoting indie.

The Old-fashioned Way

Buy their books, people, in whatever form — print, ebook, audio, or whatever. But don't just buy them. Read them. Tell everyone and their red-headed brother how much you loved them. Lend one to a friend, who might in turn buy the book as a gift for someone or tell five other people about it, who then go buy it. And here's an idea — you can give them as gifts! Put one on your book club's reading list; start a book club if you don't have one. Ask your local bookstore to order them for you. Ditto your library. Your words are powerful. Use them.

The Techie Way, but Low Techie

A. Subscribe by email to your favorite writers' blogs and newsletters. Then forward them to other people, who might also subscribe or visit your authors' websites. This connection can lead to book sales. While you're at it, follow them on all forms of social media. You can find me at my website (http://pamelahutchins.com) to subscribe and follow.

B. On Facebook, Twitter, and similar social media sites, post links to the authors' books. Or share/retweet links posted by others.

C. Everybody uses Amazon. Go to Amazon, and do several important things:

1. Visit their author pages. "Like" them. Share/tweet them. (http://amazon.com/author/pamelafaganhutchins)

If you don't know how to find their author page, then go to one of their books. If you click on their name below the title of the book, it will take you to the author page. If you don't know how to find their books, you're in trouble. Just kidding. Search for the book by name in the search box. It's in the center of the page near the top.

2. Visit every one of their books. "Like" them. Share/tweet them. Leave honest reviews, with credible ratings. Write simply and from the heart.

Not High Tech, But For The InterWeb Savvy

A. People buy books online at other retailers, too, and the best places, besides Amazon, for an indie author are Barnes & Noble (http://www.barnesandnoble.com/s/pamela-fagan-hutchins?keyword=pamela+fagan+hutchins&store=allproduct s) and Apple's iTunes and iBookstore. On B&N and in iTunes/iBookstore, you can leave a review/rating. Don't forget to share/tweet the author and book pages on your social media.

B. There's a virtual author/reader social club online, and it is a powerhouse: Goodreads (http://www.goodreads.com/pamelafaganhutchins). Join, people, join. Here, you can "fan" your author, rate and review all their books, and even add their books to your "to-read" list. By adding their books to your to-read list, you are in essence recommending to the world that they all do the same. Or at least to the world comprised by your Goodreads friends.

C. Do you Pinterest? From a page with your author's book and an image of its cover, "Pin it" and include a comment about why you love it. The power of the Pin. Do you Stumbleupon? Again, from a page with something awesome about your author and their book, stumbleit. Use any other social media you like, too.

Now I'm Talking To The Bloggers

A. Invite your author to guest post. They can whip up a custom confection for your site, or you can interview them.

B. Here's an idea: you write about their book — as in, review it. I'll bet your author friend will even give you a book for a giveaway. Don't expect expensive loot, though. Indie authors are ramen-noodle eating, Salvation Army clothes-wearing sorts of people whose kids walk uphill in snow to school, and like it.

C. Guest post on their blogs, which brings your traffic over to meet them, and potentially creates followers/purchasers.

D. Join Amazon's Associates, or B&N's Affiliate Programs and sell books for a commission on your site.

E. And of course, share/post/tweet/pin/stumble like mad over all of the posts created above.

Bonus: Here's my hyper-organized grass-roots marketing spreadsheets, for her "army," free for you to download and emulate. (https://www.box.com/s/c621f562f74e5e139ab9)

Some of you are salivating with intention and I lost others of you at the first mention of booting up your computer. That's OK. Just do the stuff you're comfortable with. It's all good.

Thanks for supporting indie authors, and me. If you want a copy of my Grassroots Army Spreadsheet, you can get one on my website under Authorpreneurship Resources (http://pamelahutchins.com/free-resources/authorpreneurship/).

SAMPLE PRESS RELEASE

FOR IMMEDIATE RELEASE

April 1, 2013

Award –Winning Author Pamela Fagan Hutchins Combines Mystery and Adventure in Upcoming Romantic Thriller, *Leaving Annalise*

Houston, TX – Award-winning author Pamela Fagan Hutchins announces the August 1ˢᵗ release of her romantic thriller, *Leaving Annalise* (ISBN 978-1939889010), the second novel in the Katie and Annalise series that continues the fast-paced adventure tale of a Texas attorney who has escaped her corporate life on the tropical island of St. Marcos. *Leaving Annalise* is the sequel to Ms. Hutchins' debut novel *Saving Grace*, the Romance category winner in the 2010 Writers' League of Texas Manuscript Competition and the Top Ghost Story winner in 2012 by the Houston Writers Guild. Ms. Hutchins moved 50,000 copies of *Saving Grace* in the first six months after its release.

In *Leaving Annalise*, one unexpected and hotly fought-over little boy, two dead bodies, and a series of home vandalisms throw Texas attorney turned island chanteuse Katie Connell into a tizzy. Juggling all of this, Bloody Mary cravings, baggage, and the bad guys too, she waffles between the jumbie house that brought her back from the brink and the man she believes is the love of her life.

The Katie and Annalise series is packed with mystery, romance, and a touch of magical realism, and provides readers with an experience that is zany, tropical, intense, and eerie, all at once. The books combine an exotic setting with vivid characterization, authentic-sounding dialogue, and real emotion, all balanced with page-turning doses of action and suspense. Hutchins captures the spirit of the Caribbean islands with captivating and imaginative stories that readers will find fun, witty, exciting, and difficult to put down.

"I spent many years on the island of St. Croix and have always wanted to write novels that capture the exotic atmosphere of the tropics," said Hutchins. "*Leaving Annalise* picks up where *Saving Grace* leaves off, when the main character, Katie, a single attorney who has found redemption in her voodoo rainforest house and romance in the islands, is confronted with the sexy Texas investigator she had fled before. As soon as Katie caves in to her feelings for him, strange things begin to happen, centered around her house Annalise and the unexpected appearance of a one-year old little boy into her life. Katie feels like she's in the eye of a storm, but she learns that, instead, she is more like the hub in a wheel, the one who must hold the center together for everyone and everything else."

Hutchins writes award-winning women's mysterious fiction and relationship humor nonfiction. A former workplace investigator, human resources executive and employment attorney, she has authored seven books, including *Leaving Annalise, Saving Grace, Hot Flashes And Half Ironmans, How To Screw Up Your Kids, How to Screw Up Your Marriage, Puppalicious and Beyond,* and *The Clark Kent Chronicles.* She is also a contributing author to *Easy to Love But Hard to Raise* and the upcoming *Easy to Love But Hard to Teach* (DRT Press), *Ghosts!* and *OMG - That Woman!* (Aakenbaaken & Kent), and *Prevent*

Workplace Harassment (Prentice Hall). Ms. Hutchins is the winner of the Parenting/Divorce category of USA Best Books in 2012 (with additional award winners in Narrative Nonfiction and Women's Health). She won the 2010, 2011, and 2012 Contemporary Fiction awards from the Houston Writers Guild, and their 2012 Nonfiction award. She won the 2010 Writers League of Texas Romance award, and the 2012 Houston Writers Guild Ghost Story award. Hutchins lives with her husband and blended family in Houston, but their hearts remain in St. Croix, US Virgin Islands.

For more information on the author or *Leaving Annalise,* please visit Ms. Hutchins' website (www.pamelahutchins.com) or her Amazon author page (**www.amazon.com**/author/pamelafaganhutchins).

For further information, please contact:

Publicist Name

Address

Phone number

Fax

Email

Website

SAMPLE REVIEW SOLICITATION LETTER

Dear Mr./Ms. Reviewer::

We are requesting consideration of the enclosed novel, *Leaving Annalise* by Pamela Fagan Hutchins, for review. We have included two copies of the book, a press release and promotional materials, and this letter, per the instructions on your website.

Leaving Annalise is the second novel in the Katie and Annalise series, by Ms. Hutchins. It is a women's fiction mystery. In *Leaving Annalise*, one unexpected and hotly fought-over little boy, two dead bodies, and a series of home vandalisms throw Texas attorney turned island chanteuse Katie Connell into a tizzy. Juggling all of this, Bloody Mary cravings, baggage, and the bad guys too, she waffles between the jumbie house that brought her back from the brink and the man she believes is the love of her life.

Ms. Hutchins is the winner of the Parenting/Divorce category of USA Best Books in 2012 (with additional award winners in Narrative Nonfiction and Women's Health). She won the 2010, 2011, and 2012 Contemporary Fiction awards from the Houston Writers Guild, and their 2012 Nonfiction award. She won the 2010 Writers League of Texas Romance award, and the 2012 Houston Writers Guild Ghost Story award. She is an attorney, workplace investigator, and entrepreneur as well as an author. She has five nonfiction books with SkipJack as well as *Leaving Annalise* and its series predecessor, *Saving Grace*. SkipJack will publish the third novel in the Katie and Annalise series in 2013.

SkipJack Publishing is a small publisher that, at present, publishes Ms. Hutchins and Helen Colin. We anticipate adding additional authors in the near future.

Sincerely,

Eric Hutchins

PUBLICIST PAULA MARGULIES'
INTERVIEW OF PFH

"Marketing and Promotion," as published on The Writer's Edge (http://writersedgeinfo.blogspot.com/), by Paula Margulies

I'm often asked by bloggers and prospective clients to talk about some of my clients' success stories. Here's one I'm happy to share: Pamela Fagan Hutchins, a Houston attorney who has written a number of nonfiction books, is experiencing great success with her first novel, a romantic thriller called *Saving Grace*. Pamela and her husband, Eric, who was once a bookstore owner, have sold over 5,000 copies of *Saving Grace* since its launch in November of 2012. They delivered an additional 33,018 copies of the book in a free download on Amazon that pushed *Saving Grace* to three weeks on the bestseller lists and netted Pamela's novel nearly 100 reviews.

Pamela has been featured in numerous print, radio, and television interviews and has given over 30 blog interviews. She has appeared at bookstores throughout Texas and will be touring nationwide with *Saving Grace* this summer.

I decided it might be better to let Pamela describe the reasons for her success in her own words. My interview with her is listed below. *-Paula Margulies*

What have you done in the way of promotion to help sell *Saving Grace*?

A LOT! Of course we did the big giveaway with Amazon's KDP Select, but we've also given away about 100 hard copies of the book to reviewers and in contests. I've done 14 book signings so far, with another 60 scheduled for this summer. I've done Q&As for book clubs, and a speech that dovetailed with the profession of my protagonist for a writers group, as well as several other speeches on general writing topics for writers groups. You mentioned the media (thank you for that, Paula!), and we even did some advertising in print media to promote some of the book signings. I also blog weekly (about 3000 views per month), and I actively engage in social media, mostly through Facebook, Twitter, and Goodreads. I entered *Saving Grace* in several contests, and was lucky enough to score some wins.

What would you say are the overriding reasons for your success with this novel?

I believe in my heart that *Saving Grace* is an enjoyable read, but my success comes mostly from the promotional efforts made by many, many other people to get some attention for this book. It's easy to remain just a needle in a haystack with over half a million books published in 2012. I indie published, which makes my book an even smaller needle, but we -- my husband and I are partnering on this indie publishing adventure -- decided to really go for it with my debut novel, including pitching the book for chain distribution with Hastings Entertainment and Barnes and Noble, as well as booking me for roughly 80 events. In the end, it comes down to good, old-fashioned hard work.

Many pundits are dismissive of authors who sell books at bookstores. Do you agree? Why or why not?

I don't agree! I've found that having a presence in book stores is important for a number of reasons. First, when I hold a book event, like a signing, I reach new readers who prefer to shop brick and mortar stores. Yes, there are still millions of diehards who refuse to give this antiquated practice up! Second, a print book placed in someone's hand has a life beyond electrons. You're making a tangible connection with a reader, who in turn can carry that book around with them where other people see it, lend it to others, or even give it as a gift. Third, placement in book stores stimulates ebook sales. I've found that most people need to see the cover of *Saving Grace* and/or my name several times before it tips them to the buying point. Seeing my book on the shelves in a store counts as one of those times, a highly-legitimizing time. My ebook sales always surge in the wake of book events.

How has the publicity work we've done together helped you? Would you recommend that other authors hire a publicist?

Paula, you've been such an important part of our marketing and promotion. You were absolutely key to achieving our goals for *Saving Grace* in its first six months. For us, this first novel is all about gaining readers for my future books. You've booked me in print, radio, and TV, gotten me events in great stores, and helped us net fantastic reviews with Kirkus and Midwest Book Review. You've placed timely and effective releases on the wires, too. Because of these things, my events exceeded our expectations, helped us gain distribution with chain stores and made this 60-city tour feasible. We've learned so much from you, too. I highly recommend working with a publicist for other authors. I didn't have the time to do what Paula did for me, nor the expertise and contacts to do it as well as her, even if I had the time.

What do you consider to be the most important advice for authors who are just starting out?

Patience, Grasshopper. Write, write, and re-write. The writing is the most important thing, and the publishing side is a sloooowwww process. Even when you get published, you need patience, because then you will have to do things outside your comfort zone to promote your book, at the same time as you keep writing. It's hard work and definitely not a get rich quick scheme, but it's so rewarding. I wouldn't trade it for any other work.

If you had to do it all over again, is there anything you would change?

Yes!! As an indie author with a debut novel, Amazon is a tremendously important venue for me. I did KDP Select Free Days very successfully. However, two weeks later, Amazon removed *Saving Grace* from KDP Select because Apple's iBookstore had not pulled the title down as I had requested through Smashwords. However, one week later I had the chance to put it back in KDP Select once Apple finally complied with the removal order, and we chose instead to experiment with ebook distribution through every available channel. My instincts told me then we were making the wrong call, and boy did it ever turn out to be a bad choice. I lost a lot of traction, sales, and rankings as a result, and we never got it back. The book has continued to do well, but it was doing amazingly well until then.

How would you describe your lifestyle since promoting this book? Do you have lots of time, or have you had to make some sacrifices to sell your book successfully?

I spend all my spare time working on book promotion and writing. I still have a day job, a husband, five kids, and four dogs, and manage to exercise, but that's about it. We no longer have any social life outside book events. The planned tour itself, while exciting, will take me away from my husband for most of the summer, which for us is a huge sacrifice (we really like each other ;-)). However, I will have one of the dogs and a revolving cast of my young adult children with me, and I treasure the thought of all the one-on-one time I will have with each of them on the road.

What are your future plans for *Saving Grace*, and do you have any other books in the works?

Saving Grace is the first novel in the Katie & Annalise series. The second novel in the series, *Leaving Annalise*, comes out in August 2013. The third novel is called *Missing Harmony*, and we will release it in February 2014. I plan to continue promoting *Saving Grace*, but in conjunction with the other two. Each will get its turn in the spotlight. And, of course, there are more books -- fiction and nonfiction -- on the horizon as well! I'll release *What Kind of Loser Indie Publishes, and How Can I Be One Too?* in August 2013, as well.

RESOURCES—BECAUSE I DIDN'T GET THIS SMART BY ACCIDENT

Here are some of the resources I recommend on the subject of indie publishing, in addition to the many others I have included in the main text of *Loser*:

- *Skip all the Jack* blog: http://skipjackpublishing.com/blog-2/

- *Author, Publisher, Entrepreneur* by Guy Kawasaki: http://apethebook.com/

- *Let's Get Digital* and *Let's Get Visible* by David Caughron, and his blog: http://davidgaughran.wordpress.com/

- *1001 Ways to Market Your Book* by John Kremer, and his website (featuring the best resources and lists ever): http://bookmarket.com

- *Self-Published Author* website (run by Bowker): http://selfpublishedauthor.com

- *Writing, Reading, and Publishing in the Digital Age*: http://janefriedman.com

- *The Writings and Opinions of Dean Wesley Smith* blog: http://www.deanwesleysmith.com/

- *A Newbie's Guide to Publishing* blog: http://jakonrath.blogspot.com/

- *Molly Greene: Writer* blog: http://molly-greene.com

ABOUT THE AUTHOR

Pamela Fagan Hutchins holds nothing back. She writes award-winning best-selling women's mysterious fiction and relationship humor books, mostly from her home in Texas, where she lives with her husband, Eric, and their blended family. She is the author of many books, including *Saving Grace, Leaving Annalise, What Kind of Loser Indie Publishes, and How Can I Be One, Too?, How To Screw Up Your Kids*, and *Hot Flashes and Half Ironmans*, to name just a few.

Pamela spends her nonwriting time as a workplace investigator, employment attorney, and human-resources professional. You can often find her hiking, running, bicycling, and enjoying the great outdoors.

For more information, visit http://pamelahutchins.com or e-mail pamela@pamelahutchins.com. To hear about new releases first, sign up for her newsletter at http://eepurl.com/iITR.

You can buy Pamela's books at most online retailers and brick-and-mortar stores. If your bookstore or library doesn't carry a book you want—by Pamela or any other author—ask them to order it for you.

BOOKS BY THE AUTHOR

Fiction from SkipJack Publishing
Saving Grace, SkipJack Publishing (Katie & Annalise #1)
Leaving Annalise, SkipJack Publishing (Katie & Annalise #2)
Missing Harmony, SkipJack Publishing (Katie & Annalise #3—coming soon)

Nonfiction from SkipJack Publishing
The Clark Kent Chronicles: A Mother's Tale of Life With Her ADHD/Asperger's Son
Hot Flashes and Half Ironmans: Middle-Aged Endurance Athletics Meets the Hormonally Challenged
How to Screw Up Your Kids: Blended Families, Blendered Style
How to Screw Up Your Marriage: Do-Over Tips for First-Time Failures
Puppalicious and Beyond: Life Outside the Center of the Universe
What Kind of Loser Indie Publishes, and How Can I Be One, Too?

Other Books by the Author
OMG—That Woman! (anthology) Aakenbaaken & Kent
Ghosts (anthology), Aakenbaaken & Kent
Easy to Love, But Hard to Raise (2012) and *Easy to Love, But Hard to Teach* (coming soon) (anthologies), DRT Press, edited by Kay Marner & Adrienne Ehlert Bashista
Prevent Workplace Harassment, Prentice Hall, with the Employment Practices Solutions attorney

CPSIA information can be obtained at www.ICGtesting.com
Printed in the USA
LVOW12s0019051113

359845LV00002B/4/P